# AMAZING
# STORIES FROM
# GENESIS

by Cindy Smith

Group
Books

Loveland, Colorado

To my dad and mom,
who taught me the value of
creativity,
and to my husband—
thanks for your encouragement.

**Amazing Stories From Genesis**
Copyright © 1992 Group Publishing, Inc.

**Credits**
Edited by Lois Keffer and Kathleen Mulhern
Cover designed and illustrated by Sam Thiewes
Interior designed by Dori Walker
Copyedited by Candace McMahan
Illustrations by Jeff Carnehl

Unless otherwise noted, Scriptures quoted from **The Youth Bible, New Century Version**, copyright © 1991 by Word Publishing, Dallas, Texas 75039. Used by permission.

**Library of Congress Cataloging-in-Publication Data**
Smith, Cindy, 1957-
    Amazing stories from Genesis / Cindy Smith
      p.   cm.
    1. Bible  O.T.  Genesis—Study and teaching. 2. Bible crafts.
    I. Title.
BS1235.5.S65  1992
222'.11'007—dc20                             92-15880
                                                   CIP

10  9  8  7  6  5  4        03  02  01  00  99  98  97  96
ISBN 1-55945-094-0
Printed in the United States of America.

# CONTENTS

# INTRODUCTION

The stories found in the book of Genesis form an important foundation for children's understanding of who God is and how he interacts with people. *Amazing Stories From Genesis* brings these exciting stories to life for third- and fourth-graders with a fascinating variety of active learning experiences. In each lesson you'll find activities that appeal to every kind of learner and learning style.

Active learning helps students understand the important biblical truths behind each story and discover how those truths apply to their daily lives. You'll enjoy seeing your students' enthusiasm as they get involved in games, simple crafts, skits, group interaction, art projects and lively stories. And you'll be amazed to see how much kids remember when, instead of just listening, they're given the opportunity to *participate*.

With each lesson you'll find the Bible basis, a simple lesson outline for your personal preparation and a list of easily obtainable supplies. Many lessons contain photocopiable handouts. Lessons range from 45 to 60 minutes, depending on the size of your class and the number of activities you choose.

*Amazing Stories From Genesis* will bring the Bible to life in your classroom and challenge your students to deepen their relationships with our amazing God.

# LESSON 1
## CARING FOR GOD'S WORLD

**Story: The Creation of the World**
**Genesis 1; 2:1-4**

Good News: God created our world and has given us the work and fun of caring for it.

The opening verses of Genesis tell the powerful story of God's creation of the universe, inviting our awe. What amazing beauty, whimsy, majesty and diversity! Best of all, the story reminds us that we are created in God's image. God has given us creativity and charged us with the responsibility of caring for the earth.

Children are fascinated by the wonder of creation—they love snails and seedlings, gerbils and giraffes. This lesson will help third- and fourth-graders appreciate the marvelous world God has given us and explore ways to care for and preserve it.

# A Look at the Lesson

1. **Kool-Aid Clay** (15 minutes)
2. **Creation Story** (5 minutes)
3. **Sidewalk Art** (15 minutes)
4. **Trash Pickup** (8 minutes)
5. **Care for Creation** (8 minutes)
6. **Thanks Circle** (4 minutes)

# Preparation

Gather supplies for Kool-Aid clay; Bibles; sidewalk chalk; a large paintbrush; a bucket of water; grocery sacks; photocopies of the "Care for Creation" handout; pencils; and a collection of natural objects such as feathers, rocks, shells and pine cones.

# 1  Kool-Aid Clay

(You'll need measuring cups and spoons, a large spoon, flour, salt, cream of tartar, an envelope of Kool-Aid, a saucepan, water, vegetable oil and a stove or an electric hot plate. You'll also need Bibles.)

Invite kids to make clay using Kool-Aid "dust." Supervise as they mix 1 cup flour, ¼ cup salt, 2 tablespoons cream of tartar and Kool-Aid powder in a saucepan. Have kids stir in 1 cup water and 1 tablespoon vegetable oil and stir over medium heat until the mixture forms a ball in the center of the pan. Remove the mixture to a floured surface and knead for one minute.

Give each child a lump of the clay. If you have a very large class, you may wish to double the recipe.

Have kids sit in a circle and look up Genesis 1; 2:1-4 in their Bibles.
Say: **Imagine a time when there was nothing on earth but water and darkness. Once the world was like that. Then the power of God came and changed everything. God began to create the world as we know it. Now it's your turn to create.**

Have volunteers read the passage aloud. Then assign a verse or section of the passage to each student. Have kids use the Kool-Aid clay to make whatever their verses name. (More than one child may be assigned a verse about fish, birds, animals or people.)

# 2 Creation Story

(You'll need the clay objects the kids have made.)

Read or tell the story from Genesis again. As each part of creation is mentioned, ask the student or students who made that part out of clay to place it in the center of the circle. Then ask:

● **How do you feel about your creations?**

● **How do you think God felt when he looked at his finished creation?** Encourage kids to use the Bible passage to support their answers.

● **How are our creations like God's creation? How are they different?**

Say: **Let's do some more creating!**

# 3 Sidewalk Art

(You'll need a sidewalk or six large sheets of newsprint, sidewalk chalk, a large paintbrush and a bucket of water.)

Take kids outside to a sidewalk. Mark off areas of the sidewalk to represent the six days of Creation. If the weather doesn't cooperate, have kids work inside on six large sheets of newsprint. Distribute the sidewalk chalk. Assign each student to draw what God created on one of the six days of Creation. Assignments may be given to individuals or groups.

Allow several minutes for drawing. Then call time and ask kids to admire each other's work. As they're looking at the chalk drawings, dip a large paintbrush into water, fling water onto one of the drawings, then brush it in, deliberately ruining the picture. In spite of loud protests, hand the brush and bucket of water to one of the students and invite him or her to ruin another drawing. Keep passing the brush and bucket until everyone has participated in ruining the drawings.

Then ask:

● **How did it feel to create your drawing?**

● **How did you feel when someone destroyed your drawing?**

● **How did it feel to destroy someone else's drawing?**

● **How was destroying these drawings like what is happening to the beautiful world God created?**

● **How do you suppose God feels about that?**

● **How can we take better care of God's creation?**

Say: **It's surprising how much we can accomplish when each person does just a little bit to care for God's creation. Let's see what we can do right here and now.**

# 4 Trash Pickup

(You'll need a grocery sack for each child.)

Take kids around the church or to a nearby park or alley that needs a good cleanup. Collect trash and sort it. Recycle what you can and dump the rest. As you work, talk about the opportunities for recycling in your community.

Ask:

● **What kinds of recycling do you do at home? at school?**

Have kids wash their hands before coming back to class.

Say: **We now have clean hands and a clean (alley, park, churchyard). Let's explore more ways to care for God's creation.**

# 5 Care for Creation

(You'll need photocopies of the "Care for Creation" handout, Bibles and pencils.)

Cut apart the handout and give each student a card and a pencil. (It's okay if more than one child has the same card.) Say: **On your card you'll find the reference for a Bible verse. Look up your verse and write it on the back of your card.**

After kids have written their verses, say: **On the front of your card you'll find an assignment to do at home this week. Different kids will get different assignments to care for various parts of creation.**

Ask:

● **What does your Bible verse have to do with your assignment?**

Say: **Next week you can tell me how your assignment went.**

If you have extra copies of the cards, invite kids to take more than one assignment.

# 6 Thanks Circle

(You'll need an assortment of natural objects such as feathers, rocks, shells and pine cones.)

Gather in a circle and ask each child to choose an object. It's okay if several students share the same object. Have kids take turns finishing this sentence: "I'm glad God made (name the object), because ..." Begin with the object you have chosen. For instance, you might say you're glad God made pine cones because they smell wonderful, they make pretty decorations or they remind you of a fun camping trip.

After each child has expressed thanks, close with prayer, thanking God for our wonderful world and asking God's help to care for and enjoy it.

Have kids take their clay creations home as reminders to respect and care for God's beautiful world and everything in it.

# CARE FOR CREATION

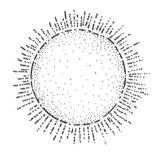

### Creation: Day 1
Look up Genesis 1:3.
A thin layer of gas all around the Earth protects us from too much sunlight. If we destroy that layer, the sun can make us sick and damage crops. Pollution from cars destroys that layer of gas. This week ride your bike or walk somewhere that your family would normally drive. Cut back on car exhaust!

### Creation: Day 2
Look up Genesis 1:9.
The more water we use, the more likely it is that one of the rivers God created will run dry, killing fish and other wildlife. A 10-minute shower uses 50 to 70 gallons of water. Challenge yourself to take shorter showers this week, but don't skimp on scrubbing!

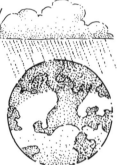

### Creation: Day 3
Look up Genesis 1:11.
Like other plants, trees help keep our air clean. They give off helpful gases and take away harmful ones. When we use paper products, we use up trees. Challenge yourself to take your lunch to school this week without using any paper products. Save a tree!

### Creation: Day 4
Look up Genesis 1:16.
Sometimes we can hardly see the stars because of all the city lights. The electric plants that power all those lights generate air pollution, too. This week give each family member 1 point every time he or she remembers to turn off a light or an appliance no one is using. Next Sunday see who has collected the most points.

### Creation: Day 5
Look up Genesis 1:20.
Cut apart plastic six-pack binders for soft drink cans before you throw them away so that sea animals don't choke on them. Make a poster encouraging others to do the same and display it in a public place.

### Creation: Day 6
Look up Genesis 1:24.
Choose one of these ideas for your own "Be Kind to Animals Week." If you have a pet, show it special attention by cleaning its living area. Or do this for a friend's or neighbor's pet. Set out water and seed for the birds. Or donate food to a local animal shelter.

# LESSON 2

## BEING FRIENDS

**Story: The Creation of Man and Woman**
**Genesis 2:7, 18-22**
Good News: God creates men, women, boys and girls to be friends.

After creating Adam, God realized that Adam was lonely. He needed another human being to share God's wonderful creation. So God created Eve. Like Adam, we long to share our lives with others. It's through relating to others that we learn about ourselves, our world and God.

Third- and fourth-graders are discovering God's plan for people to be interdependent. During these grade-school years, children learn lots of important lessons about true friendship. This lesson will help them discover how to respond to hurting friends, how to make new friends and how to maintain friendships.

# A Look at the Lesson

1. **Putting It Together** (8 minutes)
2. **The First Friends** (8 minutes)
3. **One-and-Only Lonely** (3 minutes)
4. **Partners and Friends** (10 minutes)
5. **Friendship Game** (10 minutes)
6. **Thank You Cards** (10 minutes)
7. **Prayers for Friends** (5 minutes)

# Preparation

Gather sheets of 8½ × 11 paper, large paper grocery bags, photocopies of the "True Friends" handout, pencils, markers, blank cards, envelopes, tape, sticks of gum, construction paper and scissors.

# 1 Putting It Together

(You'll need the 8½ × 11 paper.)

Ask kids to choose partners. Give each pair one sheet of paper. Say: **Keeping one hand behind your back, help your partner fold a paper airplane. Each of you can use only one hand.**

Give kids a few minutes to fold their airplanes, then ask:

● **If your partner had refused to help, could you have made an airplane with only one hand?**

● **What other fun things require more than one person working together?**

● **Think of all the things you do with other people. What if you were the only person around?**

● **How would you take care of yourself?**

● **How would you have fun?**

Say: **Let's hear a story about someone who was all alone.**

# 2 The First Friends

Invite kids to role play the story of Adam and Eve. Ask for three volunteers to play the parts of God, Adam and Eve. Ask the remaining children each to choose one animal to play. Explain that as you read the story, each child should act out his or her part. Direct the action as you read.

Say: **When the world was fresh and new, God was pleased with all the animals, delicious fruits, shady trees and rushing rivers. Then God decided to make someone really special.**

**So God took some dust from the ground and shaped a man out of it. But it was still nothing more than a lump of clay. Then God gave the clay man a great gift: God filled the man with his own breath. Then Adam came to life! He could speak and think and laugh. God brought all the animals to Adam, who had a fine time giving them their own names.** Have the animals come forward and make appropriate sounds and motions.

Say: **"My you have a long neck," Adam would say. "I think you should be a giraffe." The giraffe gracefully walked away as the elephant came forward. "And you, sir, your trunk is also very long. You shall be called an elephant . . ."** Improvise a naming sentence for each child representing an animal.

Say: **But Adam was lonely. Adam was the only human on earth. The animals were fine company, but they were not like him. Besides, Adam needed help managing the world God had made. God understood this. So one day, God made Adam fall into a deep, deep sleep.** Ask kids to close their eyes.

Say: **While Adam slept, God took one of his ribs out and made a woman from it.** Ask the children to open their eyes. **God then wakened Adam and showed him the woman. Adam said: "She's wonderful! She's a human, just like me! I'll call her Eve, and she'll be my best friend." And that's how God created the first two friends.**

# 3 One-and-Only Lonely

Give each child a large paper grocery bag. Have kids spread out around the room so no one is close to anyone else.

Say: **Put your paper bag over your head and be completely silent for one minute. Pretend you're the only person on earth. I'll tell you when a minute is up.**

Call time after a minute, have kids take off their paper bags and ask:

● **How do you think it would feel to be the only person on earth?**

● **Do you think God cared about Adam being lonely? Why or why not?**

● **Do you think God cares when we feel lonely? Why or why not?**

# 4 Partners and Friends

Say: **Friends are important to us for many reasons. Let's do something fun with the friends we have right here. Find a partner and sit on the floor back to back. Hook your arms together. Now push against each other and stand up.**

Be prepared to give assistance to pairs who have trouble getting up. When all the pairs are standing have kids give themselves a round of applause. Then have kids form a tight circle facing clockwise.

Say: **Put your hands on the shoulders of the person in front of you. On the count of three, slowly lower yourself so you're sitting on the lap of the person behind you. The person in front of you will be sitting on your lap. Ready? One, two, three!**

Children may have to practice this "circle sit" two or three times before they can perform it. After they've done a successful circle sit, ask:

● **What was alike about these two activities?**

● **How important is cooperation among friends?**

Say: **God saw that Adam needed a friend, so God created Eve. God knows that we need friends, too. But sometimes friendships run into problems. Let's explore ways to handle problems between friends.**

# 5 Friendship Game

(You'll need photocopies of the "True Friends" handout.)

Cut apart the situation cards on the handout and place the cards face down on a table. Form pairs and have each pair draw one card. It's okay for more than one pair to have the same card.

Say: **These cards can help us figure out how to be good friends. Each card tells the beginning of a story. Think for a minute about how you would finish the story on your card. Then you'll take turns acting out the stories with the endings you've chosen.**

After each role-play, ask:

● **How did you feel about the part you played?**
● **What other ways could the story have ended?**
● **What's the best ending? Explain.**

# 6 Thank You Cards

(You'll need pencils, markers, blank cards, envelopes, tape and sticks of gum. Leave the gum wrapped.)

Distribute the pencils, markers, cards and envelopes. Ask kids each to write a short note to one of their friends, thanking them for their friendship. Then have the kids tape the sticks of gum to the backs of their cards and use the markers to create pictures with the sticks of gum. For instance, kids might add arms, legs and smiley faces to their sticks of gum. Have students place the finished cards and gum in the envelopes and write the names of their friends on the envelopes. Tell the students to give the cards to their friends this week.

# 7 Prayers for Friends

(You'll need 4½×12-inch strips of construction paper, pencils and scissors.)

Give each child a 4½×12-inch piece of construction paper, a pencil and scissors.

Say: **Fold your paper in half, short end to short end. Then fold it again, short end to short end. Draw the outline of a person on your folded paper, making sure that the figure's hands and feet extend to the edges of the section of folded paper. Cut out your figure, but don't cut the edges where the hands and feet are.** (This will ensure that the cutouts remain linked when kids unfold their papers.)

When kids have opened their paper-doll chains, say: **These paper figures represent your friends. One of the best ways to care for your friends is to pray for them. On each figure write the name of one of your friends. Then choose a partner and pray together for your friends, saying a one-sentence prayer for each of the friends you've named. Take the paper dolls home and display them in your room as a reminder of the good friends God has given you.**

Close with a simple prayer thanking God for creating the first man and woman to be friends. Ask God to help kids be good friends to those around them.

# TRUE Friends

There's a new girl in your class. She seems very shy. The last few days, you've noticed that she sits alone during lunch hour. She has a different accent that some of the other kids make fun of. You decide to be her friend by . . .

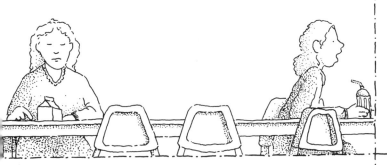

Your family has just moved. You're nervous about starting school because you don't know any of the other kids. Everyone else seems to have their own friends. You wish someone would be your friend by . . .

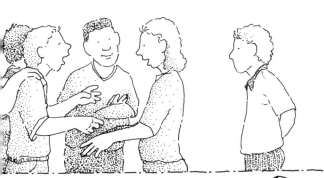

Your friend lent you a Nintendo game over the weekend. But when you get to school Monday morning, you realize you lost it somewhere on the bus. You hope your friend will . . .

Your friend borrows your bike. While she's riding it she hits a stone and crashes into a tree. When she brings back the bike it has a flat tire and a scratch. You know she didn't mean to do it. She feels bad and says she's sorry. You show her that it doesn't change your friendship by . . .

You're assigned a group science project with some of your friends. The project is to do a test to see what foods squirrels eat. You're trying to set up an experiment to find out, but one of the other kids in your group keeps goofing off and won't help plan. You remember you're his friend, so you . . .

You're feeling really angry about something that happened at home. At school you get out of control on the playground and you punch a kid who's teasing you. You didn't really mean to do it. You want to keep the kid as a friend, so you . . .

# LESSON 3
## MAKING CHOICES

**Story: The First Sin**
**Genesis 2:9, 15-17; 3:1-24**
Good News: Out of love, God gives us choices.

Genesis 3 tells the story of how sin entered the world. Adam and Eve chose to eat the fruit that was forbidden by God. As a consequence, they could no longer live in the Garden of Eden, and the close fellowship they had shared with God was broken.

Because God loves us, God gives us choices. Whether we make good or bad choices, we, like Adam and Eve, must live with the consequences. The seemingly minor choices of childhood are actually the arena for developing the ability to make wise decisions. This lesson will help kids understand the importance of the choices they make and encourage them to rely on God's wisdom to make good, loving choices.

# A Look at the Lesson

# Preparation

Gather newsprint, markers, a large piece of green plastic foam, Easter grass, scissors, construction paper, tape, toothpicks, thread, Life Savers, two twigs resembling miniature trees, miniature marshmallows, Play-Doh, Bibles, a photocopy of the "Making Choices" handout and a bowl.

# 1 Paper, Rock, Scissors

Have kids form pairs to play Paper, Rock, Scissors.

Say: **Hold one hand behind your back. Count to three together. On the count of three, show your hand. Make a fist for rock, a flat hand for paper or hold up two fingers for scissors. Rock beats scissors because a rock can smash scissors. Paper beats rock because paper can wrap up a rock. Scissors beat paper because scissors can cut paper. If you both show the same thing, it's a draw.**

Have kids play three rounds, then switch to other partners. After three more rounds call time and ask:

● **How did you decide whether you would show paper, rock or scissors?**

● **Did you usually show the same object, or did you change objects each time? Explain.**

● **How is making choices in this game like making choices in life? How is it different?**

Say: **We all have to make choices every day. Sometimes our choices are guesses—like in this game. But sometimes we have good reasons to make the choices we do. Let's think about some of the choices we have to make every day.**

# 2 / Bad Choices/ Good Choices

(You'll need three sheets of newsprint and markers.)

Ask students to think about times they have to make choices. For example, they choose which clothes to wear, which TV shows to watch and which friends to invite over.

Form three groups and give each group a sheet of newsprint. Label each sheet with a category: "At Home," "At School," "With Friends." Ask kids to list as many choices in the category on their newsprint as they can in two minutes.

After two minutes call time and ask a volunteer from each group to read the group's list aloud.

Then ask:

● **Who will be brave and tell about a time you made a bad choice?**

If kids seem hesitant, encourage discussion by telling about a bad choice you made recently.

● **What kinds of things happen when you make a bad choice?**

● **How has a bad choice hurt you? hurt your mom or dad? hurt your brother or sister? hurt your friends at school?**

Say: **Our story today is about the first two people on earth and what happened when they made a bad choice.**

# 3 / The Lost Garden

(You'll need a large piece of green plastic foam, Easter grass, scissors, construction paper, tape, toothpicks, thread, Life Savers, two twigs resembling miniature trees, miniature marshmallows and Play-Doh.)

Invite the children to make the different parts of a miniature version of the Garden of Eden. Signal the children to add their contributions to the garden at the appropriate points in the story. Assign each child (or small group) one of the following parts of the project:

● Grass—Have kids arrange the Easter grass on top of the plastic foam.

● Flowers—Have kids cut flowers from construction paper and tape them to toothpicks.

● Tree of life—Have kids hang Life Savers on branches of the twig "tree."

● Tree of the knowledge of good and evil—Have kids push miniature marshmallows onto the branches of the second twig tree.

● Characters—Have kids make five Play-Doh figures: the man, the woman, the snake and two angels.

# 4 The First Bad Choice

(You'll need the grass-covered plastic foam, flowers, twig trees and Play-Doh figures the children have made. You'll also need Bibles.)

Set the grass-covered plastic foam base in the middle of a table. Say: **God made a beautiful place called the Garden of Eden.** Have kids stick the toothpick-and-paper flowers into the base. Say: **This garden was Adam and Eve's home. In the middle of the garden, God planted two trees.** Have kids stick the tree with the Life Savers into the base. Say: **One tree was called the tree of life.** Instruct kids to place the tree with miniature marshmallows in the base. Say: **The other tree was called the tree of the knowledge of good and evil. God told Adam and Eve they must not eat any fruit from the tree of the knowledge of good and evil. God told them that if they did eat it, they would die. Let's open our Bibles and see if they obeyed God.**

Help the children find Genesis 3:1-6. Ask volunteers to take turns reading one verse at a time. Have kids place the Play-Doh figures of Adam, Eve and the snake in the garden as they are mentioned in the verses.

Continue the story by saying: **Once Adam and Eve ate the fruit, they became afraid of God. God was very sad that they had disobeyed. God called Adam and Eve before him and told them that because they had made this choice, they would have to leave** their beautiful garden. God placed angels and a flaming sword at the entrance to the garden so that they could never return. Instruct children to place the Play-Doh angels at the edge of the garden.

Say: **God told Adam and Eve that life would never be easy again. All their children would also have to make choices. Some of these would be bad choices with very sad endings.**

# 5 Choose a Corner

(You'll need the five Play-Doh figures you used for the story.)

Place each of the Play-Doh figures in a different corner of the room. (Place the two angels in one corner.) Have the children sit in the center of the room. Say: **I'm going to ask some questions about the characters in the story. You must run to the corner with the Play-Doh figure that answers the question. If the answer is God, stand up right where you are. Some of the questions might have more than one correct answer.** Make sure everyone understands the instructions. After each question, have the children return to the center of the room.

Ask:
- **Who was the first one to eat the fruit?**
- **Who told Eve that the fruit was not bad for her?**
- **Who was sad that Adam and Eve ate the fruit?**
- **Who guarded the garden?**
- **Who told Adam and Eve that they would have to leave the garden?**
- **Who made a bad choice?**
- **Who was afraid after eating the fruit?**

# 6 Making Choices

(You'll need a photocopy of the "Making Choices" handout and a bowl.)

Cut apart the cards on the handout and put them in a bowl. You don't need a card for each student.

Invite a volunteer to draw a card from the bowl, read the situation aloud and call on another student to make a decision about how to handle the situation. Have kids take turns drawing cards and responding.

After each response, ask:

- **What do you think the result of this choice will be?**
- **What is the best choice? How do you know?**
- **What general rule could you make for yourself based on the situation?** (If the situation is choosing whether to look at another student's math test, the rule might be: Don't cheat.)

# 7 Whispering the Secret

(You'll need Bibles.)

Form a circle.

Say: **Just as the snake talked Eve into making a bad choice, we can be persuaded to make bad choices. Sometimes our friends pressure us. Sometimes we talk ourselves into making wrong choices. But there is a way to make good choices. Do you want to know the secret?**

Whisper Psalm 37:3a to the child on your left: "Trust the Lord and do good." Tell that child to whisper the sentence to the next child, and so on. Ask the last child to repeat the verse out loud. Help the students find Psalm 37:3a in their Bibles and see if the sentence was repeated correctly.

Say: **When you begin to think in ways that may lead to a bad choice, remember what happens when we make bad choices. Remember that God is sad when we choose to disobey him. True happiness comes when we trust God and make choices that will please him.**

# 8 A Prayer for Life

(You'll need the garden the children made earlier and extra Life Savers and marshmallows.)

Have the children form a circle around the garden. Close by praying together for God's help in making good choices. Say: **Dear Lord,** help us remember that obeying you and following your way leads to happiness. We want to make choices that will please you. Help us to trust you and do good. Amen.

Let the children eat the Life Savers and marshmallows left over from making the two trees in the garden.

# Making Choices

HMMM...

Photocopy this handout and cut the cards apart.

Your teacher has just handed out a hard math test. You don't think you can pass it unless you get some help by glancing at another student's paper. You decide to...

Your mom asked you to clean your room. On the way to your room, you begin to say to yourself: "This is my room. I'll clean it when I'm good and ready. I don't have to do what my mom tells me." You decide to...

You're at the grocery store and see a pack of gum that has fallen on the floor. You think that maybe, since it's on the floor, it would be all right to take it. No one is looking. You decide to...

There's a new kid at school who's really nerdy. All the kids laugh at him in the hallways. Your friends are looking at you because you're not laughing. You decide to...

You stayed up late Saturday night watching a movie. On Sunday morning, you're too tired to get out of bed. You think about playing sick. You decide to...

Your best friend just told you a bad rumor about other friend. You know that if you spread this gossip, you'll be the center of attention. You decide to...

# LESSON 4
## LIVING AS BROTHERS AND SISTERS

## Story: Cain Kills Abel
## Genesis 4:1-16

Good News: God wants us to love all our brothers and sisters.

In Genesis 3 we saw the root of sin. In Genesis 4 we read about the fruit of sin. Feeling jealous and angry, Cain lashed out at his brother and killed him. Cain's actions resulted in his separation from God and from his family.

Unfortunately, our feelings of anger and jealousy separate us from our family and friends, too. You can help kids recognize these feelings in themselves and think of creative solutions. You can also help kids appreciate the good qualities in the people close to them.

# A Look at the Lesson

1. **Opposites** (10 minutes)
2. **An Angry Brother** (10 minutes)
3. **Cain or Abel?** (5 minutes)
4. **Cane and Able** (5 minutes)
5. **Brothers and Sisters** (10 minutes)
6. **A Love Gift** (8 minutes)
7. **Showing Love** (5 minutes)

# Preparation

Gather index cards, pencils, a large A cut out of posterboard, candy canes, a tape player, a cassette tape of music, a paper plate, small lunch sacks, crayons or markers, stickers, candy, slips of paper and Bibles.

# 1 Opposites

(You'll need index cards and pencils.)

Write the word "hate" on a card and keep it for later use.

Form two teams. Give each team 12 index cards and a pencil. Have each team write six pairs of opposites (such as in-out, black-white and up-down), one word per card. Have each team separate the pairs of opposites into two piles. Teams will end up with two sets of cards that can be matched by finding the opposites.

Have teams shuffle the sets of cards and give them to the other team. The first team to match all the pairs of opposites wins.

When the teams have finished, hold up your card that says "hate." Ask:

● **What is the opposite of hate?**

Say: **In today's Bible story, we're going to hear about two brothers who were opposites. One was named Cain.** Write "Cain" on the chalkboard. Say: **Cain was full of hate. The other brother was named Abel.** Write "Abel" on the chalkboard. Say: **Abel had a heart of love.**

# 2  An Angry Brother

Form two groups. Explain that group 1 will pantomime Cain's actions and group 2 will pantomime Abel's. Explain that you'll give appropriate directions to each group as you tell the story.

Say: **Adam and Eve had two children. They named the first son Cain.** *(Have group 1 stand up)* **They named their second son Abel.** *(Have group 2 stand next to group 1)* **Cain grew up and became a farmer.** *(Have group 1 pretend to hoe a garden)* **Abel decided to become a shepherd.** *(Have group 2 pretend to pet an animal)* **One day, Cain and Abel decided to bring some gifts to God. Cain had plenty of fruit, so he thought he could spare some for God.** *(Have group 1 pretend to lift up a bowl of fruit as though offering it to God)* **Abel wanted to give God something very special, so he decided to give God the best sheep from his flock.** *(Have group 2 pretend to lift up an animal as though offering it to God)*

Say: **God knew their hearts. God knew that Cain hadn't given a gift from his heart, but that Abel had given a gift of real love. God accepted Abel's gift, but he wasn't happy with Cain's gift.** *(Have group 2 smile and group 1 pout)* **Cain became very angry.** *(Have kids in group 1 stomp their feet and show anger)*

Say: **God said to Cain: "Why are you so angry? If you do good, I'll accept you."**

Say: **God warned Cain not to let his anger and jealousy turn into sin. But Cain didn't listen to God. Cain said, "Abel, my brother, come over here."** *(Have group 1 turn to group 2 and motion kids in group 2 to come close)* **Cain was so angry and jealous that he attacked Abel and killed him.** *(Have group 2 fall to the ground)* **Then Cain went back to his farming.** *(Have group 1 resume hoeing)*

Say: **God called to Cain, "Cain, where is your brother?" Cain said: "How should I know? Am I supposed to take care of him all the time?" God said: "Your brother's blood is crying out to me from the ground. Now you will be cursed in your work with the ground. You will work the ground, but it will not grow good crops for you anymore. You will wander around on the earth."** *(Have group 1 wander around the room, looking dejected)*

Say: **Then Cain said: "This punishment is more than I can stand. I will wander around on the earth, and anyone who meets me can kill me."** *(Have kids in group 1 cringe and put their hands over their heads)* **God said, "No! If anyone kills you I will punish that person seven times more." Then God put a special** mark on Cain so people would leave him alone. So Cain left God and his family.

## 3 Cain or Abel?

(You'll need a large A cut out of posterboard, a candy cane, a tape player and a cassette tape of music.)

Have the children sit in a circle on the floor. Say: **This A stands for Abel, and this candy cane stands for Cain. I'm going to turn on some music and pass the A in one direction and the candy cane in the other. When I stop the music, stop passing the items. I'll ask a question that can be answered "Cain" or "Abel." If you have the item that answers the question correctly, hold it up.**

Ask:

● **What were the names of Adam and Eve's sons?** (Cain and Abel.)

● **Which son gave God an offering of fruit?** (Cain.)

● **Which son gave God the best sheep from his flock?** (Abel.)

● **Which son became angry and jealous?** (Cain.)

● **Which son's offering made God happiest?** (Abel's.)

● **Which brother was killed?** (Abel.)

● **Who was the murderer?** (Cain.)

● **Who did God protect with a special mark?** (Cain.)

Have kids put down the candy cane and the letter A.

Ask:

● **Why do you think God accepted Abel's offering but not Cain's?**

● **Instead of killing his brother, what do you think Cain should have done?**

Say: **We know that God wants us to love each other, but it's not always easy to keep our feelings under control. Let's talk about ways we can control those feelings, and what happens when we don't.**

# 4 Cane and Able

(You'll need a candy cane for each student.)

Hold up a candy cane and write "cane" next to "Cain" on the chalkboard.

Say: **Some people use a cane because they need help to walk. A person who is physically crippled may have trouble walking. Cain's legs were fine, but his heart was crippled with anger. He let that anger ruin his life and hurt his family. When we let our hurtful feelings take control, our lives become crippled like Cain's.**

Ask:

● **When have you hurt yourself or someone close to you by letting your feelings get out of control?**

● **What were the consequences of your anger?**

Go back to the chalkboard and write the word "able" next to "Abel." Say: **Abel had a good heart. Because he loved God, he was able** (underline "able") **to love others. God warned Cain not to let his anger turn into sin.**

**Sometimes we get angry and jealous, and we might even feel out of control, but God is able** (point to "able") **to help us overcome our feelings and change our hearts. Let's be strong and loving, like Abel, so that the only canes in our lives are candy canes!**

Pass out the candy canes and let the kids eat them during the next activity.

# 5 Brothers and Sisters

(You'll need a paper plate with a happy face drawn on one side and a sad face drawn on the other.)

Have kids stay seated in a circle.

Ask children about the names and ages of their siblings. Then show the sad face. Have kids take turns coming to the center of the circle and acting out something a brother, sister or close friend does that irritates them.

When everyone has acted out an irritating behavior, show the happy side of the plate. Pass the plate around and let the children share things they like about their brothers, sisters or friends. Say: **I know it's not always easy living with brothers and sisters. But God told Cain that he could be happy if he did what was right. We can be happy, too, when we do the right things.**

Ask:

● **What are some good ways to respond when we feel like fighting?** (Talk differences over; pray together about the situation, asking for understanding and patience; ask a parent to intervene.)

# 6 ▷ A Love Gift

(You'll need small lunch sacks, crayons or markers, stickers, candy, pencils and slips of paper.)

Say: **We're going to show our brothers, sisters and friends how much we love them by making small gifts for them.**

Distribute lunch sacks, crayons or markers, and stickers. Have the children decorate the sacks and write the name of a brother, sister or friend at the top. Pass out the candy to put in the sacks. Have the children write and sign short notes of appreciation such as "I love you" or "I'm glad you're in this family" and place them in the sacks.

# 7 ▷ Showing Love

(You'll need Bibles.)

Distribute Bibles and help children find 1 John 4:7. Have the children re-form their groups from the Bible story. Form a large circle with group 1 on one side of the circle and group 2 on the opposite side. Have group 1 read the first sentence of the verse and group 2 read the second. Then have the groups switch roles and read the verse again.

Ask kids to step into the circle one by one and tell one specific way they'll show love to a brother, a sister or a friend this week. After each student speaks, have the rest of the group give a round of applause and spoken affirmations such as "All right!" or "You can do it."

After all the students have shared, have children join hands. Close with a prayer similar to this one: **Lord, help us show that we know you by loving our brothers, sisters and friends. Amen.**

# LESSON 5
## GOD'S PROMISE

## Story: Noah and the Rainbow
## Genesis 6:5–9:17

Good News: God begins a new creation and promises never to destroy all of the earth's living beings by a flood again.

*T*he story of Noah is a beautiful story of God's protection of those who love him. Noah was the only obedient man alive at one time. Because of people's extreme wickedness, God sent a flood to destroy all living creatures but saved Noah and his family. When the waters had gone down, God placed a rainbow in the sky as a sign of his promise that this watery devastation would never happen again.

God's promises are as true as God. As children grow in their knowledge of God and of his Word, they'll discover God's unquestionable integrity and be encouraged by his many precious promises. Use this story as a foundation for children's trust in God.

# A Look at the Lesson

# Preparation

Gather a bowl of animal crackers, a photocopy of the "Scripture Arks" handout, tape, newsprint, markers or colored chalk, Bibles, pencils, slips of paper, photocopies of the "Dove Promises" handout, scissors, narrow satin ribbons in four colors and glue.

# 1 Promises, Promises

(You'll need a bowl of animal crackers.)

Show kids the animal crackers. Say: **I'll give you these crackers if you jump up and down 10 times.** When the children have finished, say: **Actually, I've changed my mind. If you do five sit-ups, you can have the crackers, I promise.** After they've done some sit-ups, say: **I think I want you to do some push-ups now. I promise I'll let you have the crackers then.** Once the students have finished the exercises, say: **I think I'm just going to keep all of these crackers and eat them myself. You may all sit down.**

Let the kids express their feelings. Ask:

● **How did you feel when I failed to keep my promise?**

● **Will you have a hard time trusting me the next time I make a promise? Why or why not?**

● **What are some promises that people have made to you and kept?**

● **What are some promises that you have made? Did you keep them or break them?**

Say: **To let you know that I do try to keep my promises, here are the crackers.** Pass the bowl of crackers around. Say: **It's important that when we make promises, we keep them. Sometimes we aren't very good at that. But God keeps every promise he makes, and we can always be sure that he'll do what he says. In today's story, God makes a big promise.**

## 2 Scripture Arks

(You'll need a photocopy of the "Scripture Arks" handout, tape, eight sheets of newsprint, markers or colored chalk, and Bibles.)

Cut out the arks on the photocopy of the "Scripture Arks" handout. Have children help you tape the newsprint together on a wall, creating the format for a long mural. Set out markers or colored chalk.

Say: **We're going to tell today's story together by making a mural.** Distribute the arks equally among the students. If you have more than eight students, have them work in pairs or groups. If you have fewer than eight students, give some students two arks. Have children look up and read the scripture passages on their arks, then create drawings to describe their passages.

Allow about five minutes for students to read their passages and create their drawings. Then call time and bring everyone together. Have students explain what's happening in their drawings.

Say: **Let's explore what life on the ark was like.**

## 3 Measure the Ark

Say: **First we're going to figure out how big Noah's ark was. The Bible says it was 450 feet long. Let's walk off that distance right now.**

Beginning from church, walk approximately 450 feet in one direction. To do this, have children stretch their steps and count 150 paces. Once you have reached this distance, have the kids turn around and look back. Explain that Noah's boat was 75 feet wide and 45 feet tall. If there are any landmarks to help the children understand this distance, point those out as well. As you return to the classroom, ask:

● **What did Noah do to show that he trusted God?**

● **Do you think it was easy for Noah to obey God's command to build an ark? Why or why not?**

● **How would you have felt if you had been in Noah's shoes?**

● **In what ways was God faithful to Noah?**

● **When has God been faithful to you?**

Spark discussion on this last question by telling how God has been faithful to his promises to you.

# 4 Animal March

(You'll need pencils and slips of paper.)

Appoint two scribes and give them pencils and several slips of paper. Have kids brainstorm different kinds of animals that may have entered the ark. Have the scribes take turns writing the animals named on separate slips of paper. When kids have run out of ideas, gather the slips and have kids form pairs and stand in a line.

Say: **I'm going to pull the name of an animal from our pile. I'll assign that animal to the first pair who will then march around the room imitating the movements and sounds of that animal. When you get back to the starting point, I'll assign you another animal. We'll keep up the march until we've used up all the animals you named.**

Assign the first pair an animal. Wait about five seconds, then assign the second pair another animal. Keep sending out pairs at five-second intervals until you run out of animals.

Have kids applaud their efforts. Then ask everyone to sit on the floor as close together as possible.

Ask:

● **How is being scrunched together here like the way the people and animals on the ark must have felt?**

● **What do you think the ark smelled like after a few days of being closed up?**

Say: **God wisely planned for a ventilation system in the ark by telling Noah to make an 18-inch opening around the ark just below the roof.**

● **What kinds of thoughts do you think Noah's family might have had?**

Say: **God doesn't always put us in comfortable situations. Over** a year in a floating zoo isn't exactly a pleasure cruise! But God does promise to take care of us, no matter where we are. When we're feeling tired, discouraged or trapped in a hard situation, it's good to remind ourselves of God's promises.

# 5 Promise Bookmarks

(Before class, make enough photocopies of the "Dove Promises" handout for each student to have one dove. You'll also need scissors, narrow satin ribbons in four colors, tape and glue.)

Say: **The rainbow is a sign of one of God's promises. God makes many more promises in the Bible. Let's look at some of these promises and make bookmarks to remind us that we can trust God to keep the promises he makes.**

Give each child a dove section from the "Dove Promises" handout, scissors and a 6-inch strip of each color of the satin ribbon. Have kids cut out their doves, secure the ribbons on the inside with tape, then glue the two halves of the doves together.

After kids have finished their bookmarks, invite them to look up the scriptures printed on the doves. Ask volunteers to read their verses aloud, along with the promises paraphrased on the doves.

Ask kids each to tell one specific time or situation when it might be helpful to remember their scripture and trust God to keep his promise.

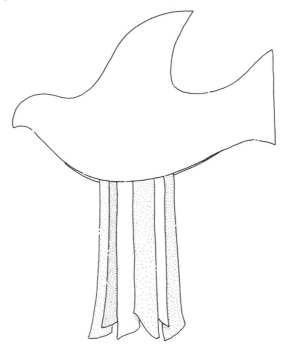

39

# 6 Prayer Promises

Say: **Promises can go two ways. God makes these wonderful promises to us. We can also make promises to God.**

Sit in a circle and invite students to make a promise to God this week. Offer simple suggestions such as treating a brother or sister kindly, doing homework on time or watching less television. Close your class with a brief prayer, thanking God for always keeping his promises and asking God to help kids keep their promises.

# SCRIPTURE ARK

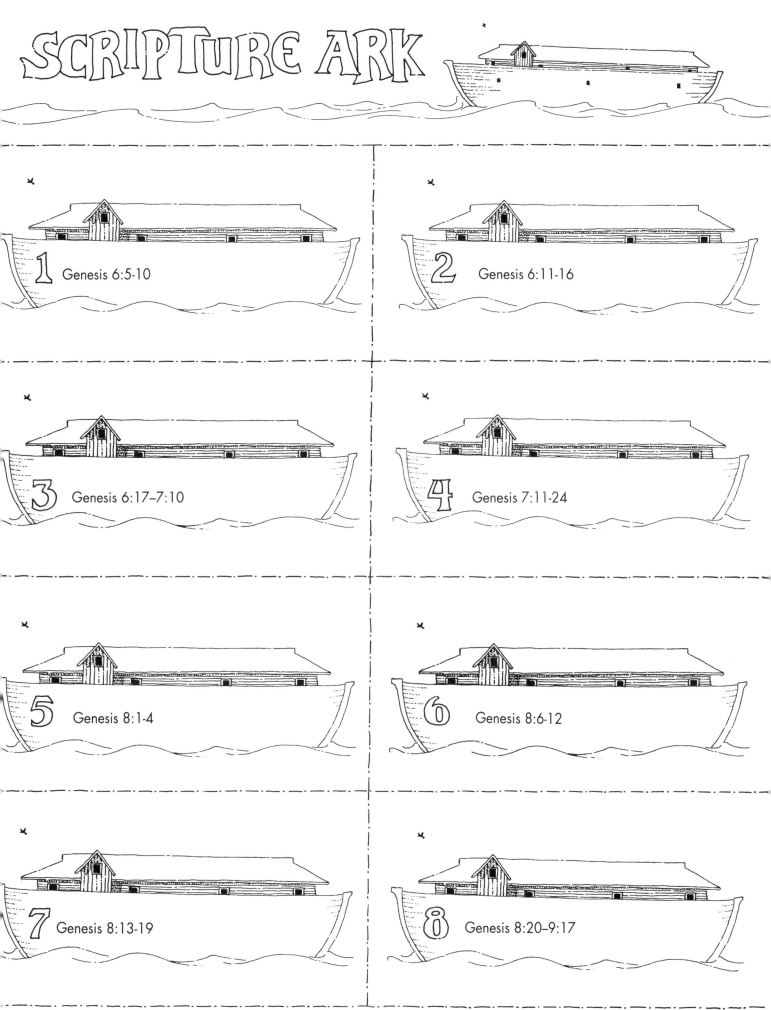

1  Genesis 6:5-10

2  Genesis 6:11-16

3  Genesis 6:17–7:10

4  Genesis 7:11-24

5  Genesis 8:1-4

6  Genesis 8:6-12

7  Genesis 8:13-19

8  Genesis 8:20–9:17

# Dove Promises

God goes with us wherever we go.

from Joshua 1:9

When we pray according to God's will,
he will answer us.

from John 14:13-14

Jesus came to give each of us a full life.

from John 10:10

# LESSON 6

## FOLLOWING GOD'S PLAN

**Story: The Tower of Babel**
**Genesis 11:1-9**
Good News: It's important to praise God for the gifts and abilities he gives us.

*I*n ancient Babylonian cities, ziggurats, or temple towers shaped like pyramids, were thought to be gateways to heaven. Babel, the Hebrew form of the name Babylon, means "gate of God."

In this story, God turns the city of Babel with its imposing tower into *balal*, which means "confused in language." What we learn from the tower of Babel story is that pride and boasting produce negative results. This lesson will help kids understand that God generously gives talents and abilities to each of us, and that God is the one who deserves praise for what we're able to accomplish.

# A Look at the Lesson

1. **Magazine Cutout** (5 minutes)
2. **Tower of Confusion** (10 minutes)
3. **Boasting Contest** (10 minutes)
4. **You're the Best** (10 minutes)
5. **Tower of Praise** (10 minutes)
6. **Prayer of Praise** (5 minutes)

# Preparation

Gather magazines; scissors; pushpins; a bulletin board; Bibles; boxes, milk cartons or assorted pots and utensils from the church kitchen; pencils; photocopies of the "You're the Best!" handout; large marshmallows; and thin stick pretzels.

# 1 Magazine Cutout

(You'll need magazines, scissors, pushpins and a bulletin board.)

As children enter the classroom, welcome them and direct them to the pile of magazines. Ask the children to cut out pictures of tall buildings. Pin the pictures to the bulletin board and talk about what it takes to construct such buildings.

Ask:

● **What's the tallest building you've ever been in?**

● **Do you like being on the top of a tall building? Why or why not?**

Say: **Today we're going to find out what happened to people after Noah's time who had big ideas about a tall building.**

# 2 Tower of Confusion

(You'll need Bibles and building materials such as boxes and milk cartons or assorted pots and utensils from the church kitchen.)

Say: **After the flood, God told Noah and his family to have lots of children and to spread all over the earth. As the years went by, the population of the world grew. But instead of filling the different parts of the world, all the people stayed together in a large group. One day, these people came up with what they thought was a great idea. Let's open our Bibles to Genesis 11 and find out what that idea was.**

Help children find Genesis 11 and ask a volunteer to read verses 1-4. Say: **What these people actually wanted to do was build a tower high enough to reach God. In a minute we'll find out if they were able to do that. First we'll build a tower of our own. As you build this tower, you'll need to talk to each other to decide how you're going to build it.**

Distribute the building materials. If your class is large, form two groups and have kids build two towers. If you use kitchen utensils, you may want to build the tower in the church kitchen.

Say: **You may begin to build. But when you hear me say the word "Babel," you may no longer say anything in English. You may speak only in silly, nonsense words while you finish the tower. Okay?** Give kids an example such as "Shwiggle woggle shwoo. Pingo pong pong pong ribbots igoo."

Let kids begin to build. Just as they're beginning to make good progress, interrupt them with the word "Babel." Allow a minute or two for the children to enjoy speaking gibberish while they build. Encourage them to discuss how to finish the tower as they're speaking only nonsense. Then call everyone together.

Say: **This is kind of like the way God handled the situation when the people were trying to build a tower to heaven.** Have a volunteer read aloud Genesis 11:5-9.

Ask:

● **How did you feel when everyone started speaking nonsense?**

● **What happened when you couldn't make each other understand what you wanted?**

● **Why do you think the people of Babel wanted to build a tower to heaven?**

Say: **The people of Babel didn't do things the way God wanted them to. They had big plans to show how great they were—but**

God caused their plans to fail. Let's come up with big plans of our own and see what happens.

# 3 Boasting Contest

Form trios. Have each trio pull its chairs in a circle.

Say: **The people of Babel thought they could become powerful and famous by building a tower that reached all the way to heaven. Now I want you to think of what you might do someday that would make you famous. Stretch your imagination and see if you can be better at bragging than anyone else in your group. Oh! One more thing. When you brag, put your hands on the heads of the other members of your trio and push them down—gently.**

Demonstrate by saying: **Someday I'm going to be famous for being the wisest teacher who ever lived.** As you speak, put your hands on the heads of two students and pull them down and forward so the students are bowing to you. Re-emphasize the need for gentleness. Then say: **Okay, we all know that I'm a terrific braggart. How about you? Start with the person in your group who's sitting closest to the door.**

After each person has had a turn bragging, bring everyone together and ask:

● **How did it feel to brag?**

● **How did it feel to listen to bragging and get pushed down?**

● **How is getting pushed down like what happens when people brag in real life?**

● **How do you think God feels when people brag?**

Say: **People who brag build themselves up by putting others down. That's just the opposite of what God wants us to do. We need to build each other up and thank God for the talents and abilities he gives to each person.**

# 4 You're the Best

(You'll need a pencil and a photocopy of the "You're the Best!" handout for each student.)

Have kids sit in a circle on the floor. Distribute pencils and photocopies of the "You're the Best!" handout.

Say: **Now, instead of bragging about ourselves, we're going to build each other up.**

Ask a volunteer to read aloud Ephesians 2:10 from the top of the handout. Have kids write their names in the center of their handouts.

Then say: **Place your paper on the floor in front of you. Now, everyone rotate one position to the left. Write on the paper in front of you one talent or ability you appreciate in that person. Or, write what kinds of "good works" God might have planned for that person in the future. Make sure that what you write is positive and encouraging.**

Have kids keep rotating until they come back to their original positions and their own handouts.

Ask:

● **How does it feel to see what everyone wrote about you?**

● **How do your feelings now compare to how you felt when you had to brag about yourself?**

● **Do you think it's important to encourage other people? Why or why not?**

Say: **We all like to hear words of appreciation. God does too! Let's build a tower of praise to show our appreciation to God for the gifts and abilities we see in each other.**

# 5 Tower of Praise

(You'll need large marshmallows and thin stick pretzels.)

Lead kids to a table. Make a pile of marshmallows and a pile of pretzels at each end of the table.

Say: **These are the building materials for our tower of praise.** Demonstrate how to use marshmallows to fasten pretzels together. **Each time you add a pretzel and a marshmallow, say, "I thank God for ..." then name a person and one of that person's abilities. For instance, you might say, "I thank God for Joe's friendliness." It's okay if you say some of the same things you wrote on the handouts.**

Have kids work together, contributing affirmations as they build. Let the tower grow as high as kids want to make it. If you have a large class, you might form two groups and build two towers.

## 6 Prayer of Praise

Have kids form a circle around the finished tower. Lead a prayer similar to the following: **Dear Lord, we praise you for the skills and abilities you've given to each person here. Help us encourage each other as we use those skills and abilities to serve you. In Jesus' name, amen.**

# YOU'RE the BEST!

"For we are God's workmanship, created in Christ Jesus to do good works, which God prepared in advance for us to do" (Ephesians 2:10, NIV).

_____
(your name)

# LESSON 7
## GOD KNOWS WHAT WE NEED

**Story: Abram Journeys to a New Land**
**Genesis 12:1-9; 13:5-18**

Good News: God leads us on a journey into a new and better world.

God called Abram to leave his home and go to a new land that God would show him. Not knowing where they were going, Abram, Sarai and Lot began their journey. Because of a disagreement over land, Lot left Abram and Sarai and chose what appeared to be the best land. Even though Abram settled for the rugged wilderness rather than the fertile plain, God promised to bless him and give to him and to his descendants the whole land of Canaan.

Third- and fourth-graders need to understand the exciting challenges that await those who choose to follow Christ. Like Abram, they may not always find the journey smooth and predictable. But they can take comfort in the fact that God will always be with them, leading them to a better, brighter future.

# A Look at the Lesson

1. **Balloon Land** (8 minutes)
2. **Leaving Home** (5 minutes)
3. **Camel Caravan** (12 minutes)
4. **Hot or Cold?** (10 minutes)
5. **Personal Adventures** (10 minutes)
6. **Prayer Adventures** (5 minutes)

# Preparation

Gather a package of medium to large balloons, Bibles, dates, raisins, crackers, a photocopy of the "Adventure with Jesus" handout, scissors, markers and newsprint.

# Balloon Land

(You'll need a package of medium to large balloons.)

As kids arrive give them each a balloon. Have kids inflate their balloons and pinch the ends so the air doesn't escape. Direct kids to form a line along one wall of the room.

Say to the first child in line: **In a minute, I'm going to tell you to let your balloon go. But first, tell me where you think it will land. Direct me until I'm standing right where you think your balloon will go.**

Continue this process with the other students. Then ask:

● **How did you feel if your balloon landed close to where you said it would?**

● **How did you feel if your balloon didn't land anywhere close to the place you chose?**

Say: **When you let a balloon go, it's hard to tell exactly where it will end up. In our Bible story today, we're going to learn about a man who started out on a journey without any idea about where he was going to end up. God said go and he went! Let's see what happened to him.**

# 2 Leaving Home

(You'll need Bibles.)

Say: **God told Abram to leave his home, most of his relatives and his friends and start life in a new land. Abram knew he'd probably never see his old home again.**

**What if you got that same order from God? Suppose you had to leave home tonight, knowing that you'd never return. Find a partner. Take 30 seconds to tell your partner what you would do to get ready to go, what you'd take with you and how you'd feel. Ready? Go!**

After 30 seconds call time and have the partners who were listeners become the speakers.

Then bring everyone together.

Ask:

● **If you had to leave this town and this country, never to see them again, what would be the hardest things to leave behind?**

Allow several students to share. Then have kids look up Genesis 12:1-5. Ask volunteers to take turns reading the verses aloud.

Then ask:

● **How do you think Abram felt about getting these orders from God?**

● **What was exciting about what God said?**

● **What was scary about these orders God gave?**

Then say: **Abram didn't have to leave *everything* behind. He loaded his belongings onto camels and formed a caravan to go to the new land God promised to show him.**

# 3 Camel Caravan

(You'll need a Bible as well as dates, raisins and crackers hidden in another room.)

Say: **Let's form a caravan of our own. Prang! I just turned you all into camels! Line up and put your front hooves on the shoulders of the camel in front of you.**

After kids have formed a line with their hands on the shoulders of the person in front, say: **Prang! I just changed you all into blind camels. Close your eyes and keep them closed. I'll hook myself**

**onto the lead camel and take us to an unknown land. Here we go—no peeking!**

Lead the caravan out of the room and up and down the halls so kids become thoroughly confused about where they are. Take a Bible with you. Have your caravan end up in front of a table where you've laid out "desert treats": dates, raisins and crackers.

Say: **It's time for you weary camels to have a snack and a rest.** As kids dive into the treats, ask:

● **How did it feel to follow blindly without any idea of where we would end up?**

● **How are those feelings like the feelings Abram probably had as he packed up his caravan and started for an unknown destination?**

Have a volunteer look up and read aloud Genesis 12:6-7.

● **The pleasant surprise we had at the end of our journey was finding these desert treats. What was the pleasant surprise Abram found at the end of his journey?** (The Lord appeared to him.)

● **How do you think Abram felt when the Lord appeared to him?** (Grateful; relieved that God was still with him.)

# 4 ▷ Hot or Cold?

(You'll need a photocopy of the "Adventure With Jesus" handout and scissors. Make an extra photocopy if there are more than 14 students in your class.)

Cut apart the seven sections of the "Adventure With Jesus" handout. Have kids form pairs. Have one person from each pair sit on the floor in the center of the room and hide his or her eyes. Give the other partners scissors and sections of the handout. Have them cut the drawings apart from the Bible verses and hide the drawings somewhere in the room. If you have fewer than 14 students, do this activity in two rounds, having partners switch roles for the second round.

When the drawings are all hidden, have the partners sit down together.

Say: **When we make a commitment to follow Christ, our lives become an adventure. We're going to look at verses and symbols to help us understand what our adventure with Jesus will be like.**

One by one, have the partners holding the verses read their verses aloud, then send the other partner out to find the hidden symbol, guiding the search by saying "hot" as the searcher gets close to the hiding place and "cold" as the searcher moves away.

After all the symbols have been found, ask:

● **What do these symbols and verses tell us about our adventure with Jesus?**

## 5 Personal Adventures

(You'll need markers and newsprint.)

Set out markers and give each student a sheet of newsprint.

Say: **Let's think about the adventures with Jesus we've had so far. Use your sheet of newsprint to draw a map of your life. Make it a path that begins with your birth and goes off the opposite end of the page to show your unknown future. Draw and write on it some important things that have happened to you, like a special birthday, a trip, an award or the birth of a brother or sister.**

Be prepared to acknowledge more difficult events as well, such as the loss of a pet, a death in the family or divorce. Give kids a few minutes to draw. Invite volunteers to share their life maps with the class. Then say: **You've had some pretty exciting adventures already! It's great to know that Jesus will be with us all along the way, leading us to new adventures.**

## 6 Prayer Adventures

Gather in a circle for a closing prayer. Ask kids if they know of any adventures now or in the future that they'd like to pray together about. For instance, some students may have music recitals they're anxious about; others may have family concerns.

Invite volunteers to pray sentence prayers about each prayer request. Then close in a prayer similar to this one: **Dear Lord, thank you for making our lives an adventure. Thank you for promising to be with us as we face the future. Help us to trust you and be willing to obey you as Abram did. In Jesus' name, amen.**

# ADVENTURE WITH JESUS

The Lord is my shepherd; I have everything I need. (Psalm 23:1).

You should be a light for other people. Live so that they will see the good things you do and will praise your Father in heaven (Matthew 5:16).

Give us the food we need for each day (Matthew 6:11).

Everyone who hears my words and obeys them is like a wise man who built his house on rock. It rained hard, the floods came, and the winds blew and hit that house. But it did not fall, because it was built on rock (Matthew 7:24-25).

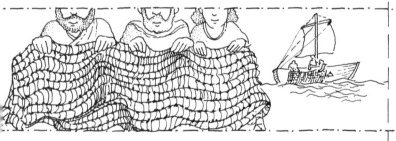

When Jesus was walking by Lake Galilee, he saw Simon and his brother Andrew throwing a net into the lake because they were fishermen. Jesus said to them, "Come follow me, and I will make you fish for people" (Mark 1:16-18).

I am the vine, and you are the branches. If any remain in me and I remain in them, they produce much fruit. But without me they can do nothing (John 15:5).

I am sure that neither death, nor life, nor angels, nor ruling spirits, nothing now, nothing in the future, no powers, nothing above us, nothing below us, nor anything else in the whole world will ever be able to separate us from the love of God that is in Christ Jesus our Lord (Romans 8:38-39).

# LESSON 8

## A SURPRISE FROM GOD

## Story: Sarah Has a Baby
### Genesis 18:1-15; 21:1-6

Good News: God surprises us; with God, nothing is impossible.

Abraham and Sarah had everything except what they wanted most—a son. Although God had promised them a son many years before, Sarah was now past the childbearing years. Abraham was 99; Sarah was 90. One day, three angels visited them with a message from God: Sarah was going to have a baby. The story of Abraham and Sarah is one of many Old Testament stories that reveal the miraculous power of God. With God nothing is impossible!

Third- and fourth-graders know all about how hard it is to wait! This lesson will help them understand the importance of trusting and waiting for God to fulfill his promises in his time.

# A Look at the Lesson

1. **Wait for This!** (5 minutes)
2. **Surprise Baby** (10 minutes)
3. **Stars in the Sky** (15 minutes)
4. **A Promise Kept** (5 minutes)
5. **New Names** (12 minutes)
6. **God's Family** (5 minutes)
7. **Prayer Hug** (3 minutes)

# Preparation

Prepare a tempting treat, such as warm cinnamon rolls or freshly baked cookies. Gather napkins, Bibles, an empty tin can for each student, nails, hammers, flashlights, nametags and markers.

# 1 Wait for This!

(You'll need the treat you prepared for the class and napkins.)

As children arrive, show them the enticing treat you've prepared. Invite them to sniff, but not to touch or eat.

Say: **I wouldn't want you to get your fingers all sticky, so I'm going to save this treat until the end of class.**

As children moan and groan, assure them that the treat will be just as delicious after class.

Ask:

● **What are some other times when you find it hard to wait?**

● **How do you feel just before Christmas or birthdays?**

● **When is it hardest to wait?**

Say: **Waiting is hard—even for grown-ups. Since I understand how hard it is to wait, I'm going to let you have this treat right now. Surprise!**

As kids eat the treat, ask:

● **Who can tell about a time you were surprised when you got something you'd been waiting for?**

Say: **Today's Bible story is about a man and woman who wait-ed a really l-o-n-g time to get something God promised them. In fact, they waited so long that they were surprised when it finally happened.**

## 2 Surprise Baby

(You'll need a Bible.)

Say: **Before we read this story, we need several characters to act out roles.**

Ask for two volunteers to stand and form an arch with their arms to make a tent. Ask for two children to be Abraham and Sarah. Have Abraham sit under the arch of the tent. Have Sarah sit behind the tent, or, if you have enough children, in a tent of her own. Ask for three children to be angelic visitors. Other children can be trees.

Say: **Now that you're all in place, I'm going to read the story. Listen carefully for your part and do just what the story says.**

Read Genesis 18:1-15 aloud, emphasizing the trees, the tent and the actions of the individual characters. Then ask:

● **What was the promise the visitor made to Abraham?**

● **How do you think Abraham felt when he heard that promise?**

● **Why do you think Sarah laughed?**

Say: **I wish I could tell you how the story ends, but you're going to have to wait, just as Sarah and Abraham did.**

## 3 Stars in the Sky

(You'll need Bibles; an empty, clean tin can for each student; nails; hammers; and flashlights.)

Say: **This wasn't the first time Abraham heard that he was going to have a child. Let's backtrack to Genesis 15:3-6.**

Ask a volunteer to read the passage aloud. Then say: **God prom-ised that there would be as many people in Abraham's family as the stars he could see in the sky.**

Ask:

● **Have you ever looked up at the stars on a clear night in a place where there are no other lights?** Encourage kids to tell about their experiences.

Say: **Let's make a starry night of our own!**

Form pairs. Give each child an empty tin can and a nail. Turn a can so the open end is down. Using a hammer, demonstrate how to pound nail holes in the top of the can.

Distribute hammers. Have kids work on a carpeted surface, outside on grass or on a sturdy table protected with layers of newspaper. Have one partner hold the can as the other makes nail holes. Encourage kids to pound the nails with great caution.

After kids have made several holes in their cans, hand out flashlights and lead the group to a room you can completely darken, such as a furnace room or a windowless bathroom. Have the children take turns shining flashlights upward through the holes in their cans. "Stars" will appear on the ceiling of the darkened room.

Ask:

● **How do you think Abraham felt as he looked at the starry sky that night and heard God's promise?**

● **How do you think Abraham felt when more time went by and he still didn't have a child?**

Lead kids back to the classroom. Say: **Thank you for being patient! Now we'll find out how God made his promise come true.**

# 4 A Promise Kept

(You'll need Bibles.)

Distribute Bibles and have students look up Genesis 21:1-6. Ask volunteers to take turns reading verses aloud. Ask:

● **What do you think it would be like to become parents when you're nearly 100 years old?**

Say: **God promised Abraham a son. Even when it seemed impossible, God made that promise come true. Let's remember to trust God to keep his promises, even when our situations seem impossible. God can do anything!**

# 5 New Names

(You'll need self-stick nametags, markers and Bibles.)

Say: **Sarah chose the name Isaac for her baby. "Isaac" sounds like the Hebrew word for laughter.**

Ask:

● **Why do you think Sarah chose that name for her baby?**

Say: **Thinking of a name for a baby is a fun and important part of being a parent. But the baby doesn't have much say in the name that's chosen. Suppose you got to choose your own name. What would it be? Quickly find a partner and work together to choose new names for yourselves.**

As partners discuss their choices of names, distribute nametags and markers. Have partners write their new names on nametags and put them on each other. Then have kids go around the class introducing themselves to one another and shaking hands. Explain that for the rest of the class, kids are to call one another by their new names.

Ask:

● **How does it feel to hear people call you by a new name?**

● **How do you think it would feel to get a new name when you're about 90 years old?**

Say: **In biblical times, names were important because they had meanings that told something about people. Sarah and Abraham were so happy to have a little boy that they gave him a name that meant "laughter." But Isaac wasn't the only person who got a name. While Abraham and Sarah were waiting for God's promise to come true, God gave them new names.**

Have kids turn to Genesis 17:3-5. Ask a volunteer to read it aloud. Say: **Abraham's name was originally Abram, which means "exalted father." God changed his name to Abraham, which means "father of many."**

Have another volunteer read Genesis 17:15-16 aloud. Say: **God changed the name of Abraham's wife from Sarai to Sarah. Both mean "princess," but when God gave her a new name, he told her she would become the mother of many nations. These new names helped Abraham and Sarah remember God's promise as they waited for their child to be born.**

## 6 God's Family

(You'll need Bibles.)

Say: **A familiar song tells how God's wonderful promise to Abraham came true. Let's celebrate God's faithfulness by singing "Father Abraham."**

After singing the song, say: **Through Isaac, Abraham became the father of all the Jews. The Bible tells us that if we put our faith in Christ, we too can be counted in God's family.**

Have volunteers look up and read Galatians 3:29 and 2 Corinthians 5:17.

Say: **God is ready to give us something better than new names—he's ready to make us "new creations" when we put our faith in Christ.**

Be sensitive to children who may want to know more about receiving Christ and becoming part of God's family. Offer to stay after class and talk with children who have further questions or would like you to pray with them.

## 7 Prayer Hug

Say: **I bet you've heard of a bear hug, but have you ever heard of a *prayer* hug?**

Have kids form a circle and put their arms around each other's shoulders. Close with a prayer similar to this one: **Dear Lord, thank you for keeping your promise to Abraham. Help us to keep trusting you, even when it's hard to. And thank you for giving us the opportunity to be part of your family. In Jesus' name, amen.**

# LESSON 9
## NARROW ESCAPE

**Story: Lot and His Family Escape**
**Genesis 18:20-33; 19:1-29**

Good News: God answers our prayers for mercy and forgiveness.

Lot and his family were living in the wicked city of Sodom. Because of the sinfulness of its inhabitants, God decided to destroy Sodom. Yet God spared Lot and his family because of Abraham's prayers. Lot's wife, however, disobeyed the angel's command not to look back; she turned into a pillar of salt.

This story offers a powerful lesson on the importance of prayer. God works through our prayers, whether we are adults or children. Third- and fourth-graders need to understand that because God is merciful and forgiving, their prayers *can* make a difference.

# A Look at the Lesson

1. **M&M's Mercy** (5 minutes)
2. **How Many?** (8 minutes)
3. **A Mission of Mercy** (12 minutes)
4. **Run Away!** (5 minutes)
5. **Prayer Power** (15 minutes)
6. **M&M's Prayers** (5 minutes)

# Preparation

Arrange for an adult helper to assist with the opening activity. Gather a large bag of M&M's candy, a plastic bag, a clear jar, a towel, tape, newsprint, markers, a metal wastebasket, matches, Bibles, scrap paper, pencils, photocopies of the "Prayer Power" handout, 3×5 cards and glue.

# 1 M&M's Mercy

(You'll need a large bag of M&M's candy, a plastic bag, a clear jar and an adult helper.)

Before class, take out the yellow M&M's, put them in a plastic bag and set them out of sight. Pour the rest of the M&M's into a jar. Put one yellow M&M's candy into the middle of the other M&M's so that it can't be seen. When it's time for class to begin, have your helper come in carrying the jar of M&M's. Improvise a dialogue similar to the following:

Helper: **Here are the M&M's you asked for.**

Teacher: *(Take the jar and scrutinize it carefully)* **I don't see any yellow ones in here. Throw it in the trash.** *(Hand the jar back to the helper)*

Helper: *(Look carefully at the jar)* **Will you keep these M&M's if there are 50 yellow ones in the jar?**

Teacher: **Yes, I'll keep them if there are 50 yellow ones.**

Helper: **How about if there are 45? Will you keep the M&M's if there are 45 yellow ones?**

Teacher: **Yes, I suppose I will keep them if there are 45 yellow ones.**

Helper: **Well, what if there are only 30 yellow ones? Will you throw the whole jar away if there are 30?**

Teacher: **No, I won't throw it away if 30 yellow ones are in there.**

Helper: *(Once again, examine the jar slowly and speak hesitantly)* **Maybe there are only 20 yellow ones in here. Will you trash this jar of M&M's if there are only 20?**

Teacher: **No, I guess not. I'll keep it if there are 20.**

Helper: *(Inspect the jar further, shaking it a little)* **Just one more question and then I'll stop. What if we only find 10 yellow M&M's?**

Teacher: **For the sake of the 10 yellow ones, I won't throw away the rest of them.**

Helper: *(Set the jar down on a table and walk out of the room)*

Say: **Today we're going to talk about one of the scariest, most exciting stories in the Bible. Remember what happened with this jar of M&M's as we begin.**

## 2 How Many?

(You'll need the jar of M&M's and a towel.)

Say: **Abraham's nephew Lot lived in a town called Sodom. One day the Lord told Abraham that the people who lived in the town of Sodom were very wicked. They were so wicked that God decided to destroy the city. Abraham loved Lot and wanted to get him out of Sodom before God destroyed it.**

**So Abraham asked God: "Will you destroy both the good and the bad? Suppose you find 50 innocent people in the city. Will you destroy it then?"**

Ask:

● **What do you think God said?** Encourage the children to give an answer based on the M&M's illustration. (No, I won't destroy it.)

Say: **Then Abraham asked God: "What if there are only 45? Will you still destroy the city?"**

● **What did God say?** (No, I won't destroy it.)

**Abraham said: "Don't be angry. Please let me speak again. What if only 30 innocent people are there?"**

65

● **And God said?** (No, I won't destroy it.)

**Abraham asked again, "Suppose there are only 20?"**

● **And God said?** Let the children answer again.

**Finally Abraham said: "Let me just ask one more time. What if only 10 innocent people are found in Sodom?"**

● **What do you think God replied?** Affirm the students' answer.

Dump the jar of M&M's on a towel. Pick out the yellow one. Ask:

● **How many innocent people do you think God found?** Let the children guess. Set the candy aside for later.

# 3 ▷ A Mission of Mercy

(You'll need tape, a large sheet of newsprint, markers, a metal wastebasket, matches and Bibles.)

Ask kids to tape the sheet of newsprint to the wall. Set out markers. Have kids work together to draw the city of Sodom. First, appoint two children to draw a wall running all around the city. Then invite other kids to quickly add three or four houses each.

Say: **Now that we have our city, let's continue with the story. God sent two angels to Sodom. There weren't even 10 innocent people in the town, so God decided to destroy the city. But, in answer to Abraham's prayers, God sent angels to rescue Lot.**

**The angels said to Lot: "Get your family together. The people in this city are so wicked that God has decided to destroy the city."**

**Lot ran out to find the men his daughters planned to marry. He said to them: "Hurry! Come with me! The Lord is about to destroy this city." But they thought he was joking.**

**At sunrise, the angels said to Lot: "It's time to go! If you don't leave, you and your family will be destroyed with the rest of the people here." Lot didn't really want to leave his home. So finally the angels grabbed his hand and pulled him and his family away from the city.**

**Then the angels said: "Run for your lives! Don't look back and don't stop. Run to the mountains or you will die!" Lot begged them, saying: "No, I'm too old! I can't make it to the mountains. Let me hide in that little village over there." The angels agreed, and Lot and his family ran to the village.**

**When the sun came up, the Lord sent fiery rain and smoke down on Sodom. The city burned. Lot's wife wanted one last**

glimpse of her old home, so she disobeyed the angels' instructions and turned around for a peek. Instantly, she turned into a pillar of salt. But God showed mercy to Lot and his daughters and allowed them to escape safely because of Abraham's prayers.

Have the children help you take down and crumple their drawing of Sodom. Stuff the crumpled paper into a metal wastebasket. Have kids follow you as you carry the wastebasket outside. Light a couple of matches and throw them into the wastebasket. Watch in silence as the paper burns. Then return to your classroom and ask:

● **How did you feel as you watched our drawing burn?**

● **How are those feelings like what Lot must have felt when the town where he had lived was burning?**

● **Why do you think God let Lot and his daughters escape?**

Have kids check their response by reading Genesis 19:29.

Say: **This story shows us that our prayers *can* make a difference in people's lives! It also shows us the importance of obedience.**

# 4 Run Away!

(You'll need a wastebasket and a sheet of scrap paper and a pencil for each student.)

Place a large wastebasket at one end of the room.

Say: **God answered Abraham's prayer by sending angels to rescue Lot.**

Ask:

● **But what did Lot have to do?**

Say: **Lot and his family had a narrow escape. In fact, Lot's wife didn't make it!**

● **What did she do wrong?**

Say: **Sometimes when we're praying, or when other people are praying for us, we realize that God is giving us a warning. The angels warned Lot that God was going to destroy the city. But Lot had a hard time obeying—the angels actually had to take him by the hand and pull him away. Then they told Lot and his family to run for their lives and not to look back. When Lot's wife looked back, she lost her life. When God gives us a warning, we need to pay attention and run for our lives, too.**

Ask:

● **What kinds of things does God warn kids about today?** (Lying; taking drugs; cheating; watching yucky movies or TV shows.)

Say: **When God warns us to run from something that's bad for us, we need to obey him right away! We need to turn away from things that could harm us and go forward toward Jesus and the things God wants us to do.**

Distribute paper and pencils. Say: **On your paper write one thing that God wants you to run from. As soon as you've finished writing, wad up your paper and toss it in the wastebasket. Then "run for your life" to the other end of the room!**

When kids are gathered at the opposite end of the room, say: **We often pray for guidance and protection for ourselves and for other people. When we pray, God lets us know what to do, but he still leaves us with choices. After God has let us know what to do, it's important to obey quickly! Now let's discover some other things about the power of prayer.**

## 5 / Prayer Power

(You'll need pencils, photocopies of the "Prayer Power" handout and Bibles.)

Distribute pencils, photocopies of the "Prayer Power" handout and Bibles. Have kids form trios. Assign each trio one or more of the five "What the Bible says" sections of the handout. If you have a large class, it's okay to assign each section to more than one trio.

Allow several minutes for trios to read and discuss their verses and complete the sentences at the bottom of the handout. Then bring everyone together. Encourage kids to share their discoveries and insights with the class.

## 6 / M&M's Prayers

(You'll need markers, 3×5 cards, glue and the bag of yellow M&M's.)

Ask:

● **What did Abraham do for Lot that helped save Lot's life?**
● **What do we need to do for the people we care about?**

Distribute markers and 3×5 cards. Set out glue. Have kids write the word "pray" in big capital letters on their cards.

Say: **God listens when we pray for people. God shows mercy to people today, just as he did to Lot. God is always willing to forgive people when they ask. He gives everyone a fresh start when they trust in Jesus.**

Hold up the bag of yellow M&M's. Say: **Think of people you know who need to accept God's help and forgiveness. For each person you think of, glue a yellow candy onto your card.**

Encourage kids to keep their cards as reminders to pray for their friends and family members who need God's mercy and forgiveness.

Have kids stand in a circle with their finished cards held in their open palms. Close with a brief prayer: **Thank you, Lord, that you always want to show mercy. Help us to be people who pray, knowing that you always hear us. Amen.**

Enjoy the remaining M&M's with your class.

# Prayer POWER

Each person in your trio will look up one of the Bible verses from the section you've been assigned. Discuss each verse with your trio, then write in your own words something you learned from the verse you read.

1. What the Bible says: Deuteronomy 4:7; Luke 18:1; Colossians 4:2.

What I learned: _____

_____

2. What the Bible says: 1 Samuel 12:23; Matthew 7:7-11; 1 Thessalonians 5:16-18.

What I learned: _____

_____.

3. What the Bible says: 1 Chronicles 5:20; Matthew 5:44; James 5:13.

What I learned: _____

_____

4. What the Bible says: Matthew 6:5-6; Ephesians 6:18; 1 Peter 4:7.

What I learned: _____

_____

5. What the Bible says: Matthew 6:7-8; Philippians 4:6; 1 Peter 3:12.

What I learned: _____

_____

Finish the following sentences, then share what you wrote with the other members of your trio.

God answered my prayer for _____

One prayer I'm still waiting for God to answer is _____.

# LESSON 10
## GOD CARES WHEN WE HURT

**Story: Hagar and Ishmael in the Desert**
**Genesis 16:15-16; 21:9-20**

Good News: God hears us when we cry and takes care of us.

When Sarah saw Ishmael mocking Isaac, she demanded that Hagar and her son be sent away. After receiving God's assurance that Ishmael would prosper, Abraham supplied Hagar and Ishmael with food and water and sent them on their way. When the water was gone, Hagar and Ishmael sat down to die. But God heard their cries and saved them.

Children know that God is great and mighty, but they often need to be reminded that God cares about every problem, no matter how large or small. No matter the source of tears, God cares and is ready to comfort and help.

# A Look at the Lesson

1. **Love and Care** (10 minutes)
2. **God Cares** (10 minutes)
3. **Well in the Desert** (5 minutes)
4. **How Sad?** (10 minutes)
5. **Teddy Bear Hug-Around** (5-10 minutes)
6. **Now Hair This** (10 minutes)

# Preparation

Arrange to have an adult helper bring a pet, such as a dog, guinea pig or hamster, to visit your class. Also bring a treat that the pet would enjoy. Hide an ice chest full of canned soft drinks and ice under a blanket somewhere in your classroom. Gather Bibles, peanut butter, saltines, blunt knives, an onion, a cutting board, a sharp knife, pencils, photocopies of the "How Sad?" handout, and a teddy bear or other stuffed animal.

# 1 Love and Care

(You'll need an adult helper, a pet and a treat the pet would enjoy.)
Say: **We have a special guest in our class today.**

Have the adult helper bring out the pet and allow children to take turns petting and playing with it. Explain that the pet may not be comfortable with a lot of attention at once, and encourage children to be gentle. Invite one of the children to give the pet a treat.

Ask:

● **What do you think (name of pet's owner) does to keep (name of pet) healthy and happy?**

● **Why does (name of pet's owner) go to so much trouble to take care of (name of pet)?**

● **What would happen if (name of pet's owner) didn't give (name of pet) all this care and attention?**

● **How is the way we care for our pets like the way God takes care of us?**

72

Say: **It's fun to have pets, but it's a big responsibility. If we love our pets, we really don't mind the work involved in taking care of them. Just as we love and care for our pets, God loves and takes care of us. Today's story is about two people who thought God didn't care about them anymore. Let's find out what happened to them.**

Have the adult helper take the pet away so children won't be distracted by it as you proceed with the lesson.

## 2 God Cares

(You'll need Bibles.)

Say: **Today's story is about Hagar and her son. Hagar was one of the slaves in Abraham's household. She and Abraham had a son named Ishmael. About 14 years later, Sarah had Isaac. Baby Isaac got special treatment because his mother, Sarah, was Abraham's wife. Ishmael's mother was still a slave, so Ishmael was a slave, too.**

**Sarah was very proud of the son God had given her in her old age. Sarah worried that Ishmael might get more of Abraham's attention than Isaac did. One day Sarah discovered Ishmael making fun of Isaac. That made her very angry. Let's see what happened next.**

Help children find Genesis 21. Ask volunteers to read verses 9-20, each student reading one verse. Ask:

● **Why did Sarah want to get rid of Hagar and Ishmael?**

● **How do you think Abraham felt about sending Ishmael away?**

● **How do you think Hagar and Ishmael felt when they were sent off into the desert and told they couldn't come home again?**

● **Sarah didn't care at all what happened to Hagar and Ishmael. Did God? How do you know?**

# Well in the Desert

(You'll need peanut butter, saltines, blunt knives and the ice chest full of canned soft drinks and ice you've hidden under a blanket.)

Say: **Abraham gave Hagar and Ishmael food before he sent them on their way. He probably *didn't* give them peanut butter and crackers, but that's what we're going to use to represent the food he gave them.**

Set out the saltines, peanut butter and knives. Encourage kids to help themselves. As kids enjoy the treat, discuss the story with them. Ask:

● **What didn't Sarah want Isaac to share with Ishmael?**

● **Why do you think Ishmael might have been making fun of Isaac?**

● **What does it feel like when people make fun of you just because they're older than you are?**

● **How do you think Hagar and Ishmael felt when they ran out of water in the desert?**

By now children should be very thirsty from their peanut butter and saltine snacks. Ask:

● **Can you remember a time when you were super thirsty and you couldn't get a drink? What was it like?**

Give students a chance to share their experiences. Then say: **I want you all to close your eyes and think really hard about what it's like to be thirsty. Keep your eyes closed until I tell you to open them.**

Ask:

● **What did Hagar and Ishmael do when they ran out of water?**

● **Who heard their cries?**

● **What did God do?**

Quietly drag the ice chest to the center of the room and open it. Say: **Open your eyes and see what I have for you! Help yourselves.**

As children enjoy their soft drinks, ask:

● **How is what I did for you like what God did for Hagar and Ishmael? How is it different?**

● **How do you think Hagar felt when God showed her the well?**

Say: **We all have times when we feel sad or hopeless. Sometimes it even feels like God doesn't care about us anymore. But God *does* know what we're going through and he *does* care for us!**

# 4 How Sad?

(You'll need an onion, a cutting board, a sharp knife, pencils and photocopies of the "How Sad?" handout.)

Say: **Different people become sad for different reasons.** Ask:

● **What was Hagar's reason for crying?**

Say: **I'm going to give us all a reason to cry—but don't worry—it won't be as bad as what happened to Hagar.**

Bring out the onion, cutting board and knife. Ask kids if they can guess what you're going to do. Cut several slices of onion, then pass it around on the cutting board and challenge kids to take a deep sniff. Ask kids to raise their hands if they have tears in their eyes.

Say: **That was just kind of silly and fun. But when you're really sad and crying, it's no fun at all! Let's explore some of the things that make us sad.**

Distribute a pencil and a photocopy of the "How Sad?" handout to each child.

Say: **Read each situation on the list. If the situation wouldn't bother you at all, put a 0 beside it. If it would make you really sad, put a 5 beside it. If it would make you just a little sad, put a 1, 2 or 3 next to it.**

Give students two or three minutes to complete the handout. Then call everyone together. Read the situations one by one and have kids call out the numbers they wrote down. Find out which situation, if any, got the most fives.

# 5 Teddy Bear Hug-Around

(You'll need a teddy bear or other stuffed animal.)

Have kids sit in a circle. Hug the teddy bear and say: **God cares when we're sad and hurting. We can pray and tell God how we're feeling, and he will comfort us. We can also comfort each other. Giving comfort is an important thing we do in God's family. When I'm feeling really sad, I like it when people (tell how you like people to respond).**

Pass the teddy bear to the next person and have him or her finish this sentence: "When I'm feeling really sad, I like it when people . . ."

(You'll need Bibles.)

Say: **There's an interesting scripture passage that tells how much God cares for us. Let's find it and read it aloud together.**

Distribute Bibles and have kids look up and read Luke 12:6-7.

Then say: **Find a partner. Choose a spot that's about an inch square on top of your partner's head. In two minutes, try to count all the hairs in that square inch.**

After two minutes call time and have partners switch roles. After two more minutes bring everyone together. Ask:

● **How many hairs did you count?**

● **Was anyone able to count all the hairs in that square inch?**

● **How does it make you feel to know that God cares about you so much that he even knows how many hairs are on your head?**

Form a circle and have kids hold hands during your closing prayer: **Dear Lord, thank you for caring about us, even when we feel sad and forgotten. Help us trust you in our sad times and show your love and comfort to others. In Jesus' name, amen.**

Write a number from 0 to 5 to show how each of these situations would make you feel. Zero means it wouldn't bother you at all; 5 means it would make you really sad.

_____ Your best friend moves away.

_____ Your bike is stolen.

_____ A good friend has a party but doesn't invite you.

_____ You stub your toe.

_____ Your pet runs away.

_____ Your mom and dad have a fight.

_____ Someone makes fun of what you're wearing.

_____ You fail an important test.

_____ You try really hard in soccer but still play poorly.

_____ Your parents can't afford the expensive shoes you want.

# LESSON 11
## A TEST OF FAITH

**Story: God Spares Isaac**
**Genesis 17:1-8,19; 22:1-19**

Good News: We can have faith that God will keep his promises.

There came a time when God tested Abraham. God told Abraham to sacrifice his promised son, Isaac. Because God had told Abraham that the covenant would extend to Isaac, Abraham trusted God completely—even to the point of trusting God's ability to raise Isaac from the dead.

The Bible tells us that we are to follow in the steps of Abraham's faith (Romans 4:12). Abraham was fully assured that what God promised, God was able to perform (Romans 4:20-21). This lesson will help build kids' faith so that, like Abraham, they can trust God to keep his promises.

# A Look at the Lesson

1. **Bash It or Not?** (10-15 minutes)
2. **Do You Trust Me?** (10 minutes)
3. **No Dough** (5-10 minutes)
4. **Real Dough** (5-10 minutes)
5. **Tug of Faith** (10 minutes)
6. **Abraham's Kids** (5 minutes)

# Preparation

During the week, call two or three students and ask them each to bring a favorite possession to show their classmates. If your class is small, you might want to contact all the students. You'll also need a baseball bat, a marker, newsprint, Bibles, a photocopy of the chocolate-oatmeal cookie recipe, ingredients for the cookies, measuring utensils, an electric skillet or access to a stove, a large spoon for stirring, a plastic bag and a sturdy rope at least 12 feet long.

# 1 Bash It or Not?

(You'll need students' favorite possessions and a baseball bat.)

Have students take turns telling about their favorite possessions. Encourage kids to explain what makes each item special.

After kids have shared, ask them to stand behind their possessions. Go up to one student, hand him or her the baseball bat and say: **I want you to smash this favorite possession of yours.**

If the student protests or questions you, just say: **I want you to smash it. That's all.** If the student refuses, take the bat and go on to the next student with the same instructions. If any of the students actually raises the bat to smash a possession, stop him or her by grabbing the bat.

When you have challenged each student, have everyone sit down. Say: **You may be a little confused by the activity we just did. That's okay. Just trust me. Pretty soon you'll see how this ties into today's Bible story.**

# 2 Do You Trust Me?

(You'll need a marker, a sheet of newsprint and Bibles.)

Say: **In today's story, God asked Abraham to do a very hard thing, something Abraham couldn't understand at all. As we read the story from the Bible, imagine what Abraham and Isaac must have been feeling.**

Write "feelings" in large letters across the top of a sheet of newsprint. Each time you ask a question about feelings, have a different student record the responses on the newsprint.

Have kids look up Genesis 22:1-2. Ask a volunteer to read it aloud. Ask:

● **How do you think Abraham felt?**

Have another volunteer read verses 3-8. Ask:

● **Now how do you suppose Abraham was feeling?**

● **Isaac wasn't a baby anymore. How do you think Isaac felt?**

Have another student read verses 9-10. Ask students again about Abraham's and Isaac's feelings. Pause to record feelings after reading verses 11-14, then again after verses 15-19.

● **Did Abraham let his feelings keep him from trusting and obeying God? How can you tell?**

● **How were Abraham's feelings like the feelings you had when I asked you to hit your favorite possessions with a baseball bat? How were they different?**

● **Do you think I ever really planned to have you smash your favorite possessions? Why or why not?**

● **Do you think God ever really planned for Isaac to be killed? Why or why not?**

● **Why do you think God asked Abraham and Isaac to go through this experience?**

Say: **God wants to have our trust and obedience in every situation. Sometimes we may wonder what's going on and why God is asking us to do hard things. But if we trust God and do what he wants us to do, things will always turn out for the best.**

(You'll need a photocopy of the chocolate-oatmeal cookie recipe, ingredients for the cookies, measuring utensils, an electric skillet or access to a stove, a large spoon for stirring and a plastic bag. If you have students who don't eat chocolate, consider making Rice Krispies Treats instead.)

Say: **When Abraham and Isaac got back from their experience on the mountain, they must have been hungry and tired. I'm feeling kind of hungry myself. Let's whip up a batch of cookies!**

### CHOCOLATE-OATMEAL COOKIES

Melt together in a large skillet:
1 ½ cups sugar
1 stick margarine
1 teaspoon vanilla
5 tablespoons cocoa
½ cup milk

Stir in ½ cup peanut butter and 3 cups oatmeal. Place rounded tablespoons of the mixture on waxed paper. Let cool.

Permission to photocopy this recipe granted for local church use.
Copyright © Group Publishing, Inc., Box 481, Loveland, CO 80539.

Hand the recipe to a student and ask him or her to read it to you. As the student reads the ingredients, intentionally ruin the cookies by ignoring the amounts given in the recipe, saying things such as "I really think it needs a lot more of this," and "We don't need *that* much."

Have kids take turns mixing the dough.

Then say: **Yuck! These cookies look horrible. Why did they turn out so badly?**

Ask kids to give their opinions about why the cookie dough was ruined. Then say: **Okay. I guess we'd better start over.**

Have children help you pour the ruined dough into a plastic bag.

# 4 Real Dough

(You'll need all the items used in the previous activity except a plastic bag.)

Ask another student to read the recipe. This time, have kids take turns carefully measuring and mixing each ingredient. Set the finished cookies aside to cool.

Say: **There! That's better! We'll be able to enjoy these cookies in just a few minutes.**

Ask:

● **Why is it so important to follow the directions in recipes?**

● **How is following the directions in a recipe like following the directions God gives us in the Bible? How is it different?**

● **Why was it important for Abraham to follow God's directions, even if he didn't understand them?**

Say: **We need to remember that God can see and understand many things we can't. God knew about the angel he would send to stop Abraham from killing Isaac. God also knew that he would provide a sheep for the sacrifice. Abraham didn't know any of these things. What he *did* know was that he could trust God.**

# 5 Tug of Faith

(You'll need Bibles and a rope at least 12 feet long.)

Say: **God promised Abraham over and over again that he would have many descendants and that Isaac was the key to that promise.**

Ask:

● **If Abraham had actually sacrificed Isaac, how would God have kept his promise?**

Invite students' speculation.

Then say: **We can find the secret of Abraham's faith in the book of Hebrews.** Distribute Bibles, have kids look up Hebrews 11:17-19, and ask a volunteer to read the passage aloud.

Then ask:

● **What did Abraham believe about God?**

● **How did this belief make it possible for him to consider sacrificing Isaac?**

Say: **Abraham had one thing that we all need: faith.**
Ask:

● **What is faith?**

Invite students to share their ideas. Then say: **We can find a defini-tion of faith in this same chapter of Hebrews, in verse 1.** Ask a volunteer to read verse 1 aloud, then ask:

● **What was Abraham sure of?**

● **Do you think Abraham could see the many descendants that God had promised?**

● **How did Abraham get his strong faith?**

● **How do we get faith?**

Invite children's responses. Then say: **Let's try something that demonstrates how faith grows.**

Have three children grasp one end of the rope. Choose one child to grasp the other end. Say: **On the count of three, pull! One, two, three!** Ask:

● **How can we add strength to the weaker end?**

Add another child to the end with only one child, then give the sig-nal to pull again. Ask:

● **This end is getting stronger, but what more can we do?** Continue adding children one at a time, until the end that started out with one child has more children than the other end. Give the one-two-three signal after each child is added.

Say: **Growing in faith is kind of like this tug of war. Every time we trust God and he *does* care for us and keep his promise, it's like adding another person to the end of the rope. Each time God cares for us, our faith gets stronger and stronger.**

● **What are some of the promises to Abraham that God had kept?** (God led Abraham to a new land, rescued Lot from Sodom, gave Abraham and Sarah a son in their old age and took care of Ishmael in the desert.)

Say: **By the time God asked Abraham to sacrifice Isaac, God had kept so many promises that Abraham knew God would take care of this situation, too.**

(You'll need the rope used in the previous activity and the cookies from the Real Dough activity.)

Say: **God's promise to Abraham came true. His descendants, the Jews, live all over the world. The Bible says that all the world will be blessed because of Abraham. And so we are, for Jesus was a descendant of Abraham. In Romans 4, the Bible says that we are children of Abraham when we live by faith.**

Ask: **How can we live by faith?** (By reading the Bible and obeying what it says; by praying about our problems and trusting God to take care of us.)

Sit in a circle and have everyone hang on to the rope. Close with a prayer similar to this one: **Lord, thank you for keeping your promises. Help us to trust you and obey you in everything. We believe that you will always love us and take care of us. In Jesus' name, amen.**

Invite kids to enjoy the cookies they made during the Real Dough activity.

# LESSON 12

## GOD GUIDES US

**Story: Choosing a Wife for Isaac**
**Genesis 24**

Good News: When we pray, God gives us guidance.

When Isaac was ready to marry, Abraham sent a servant back to his hometown to find a wife for his son. The servant, knowing he was entrusted with an important decision, prayed to God for help. When Rebekah spoke, the servant knew that his prayer had been answered.

Parents make most of the important decisions for their children. However, even the day-to-day decisions that children face can seem overwhelming. Children need to discover that when they pray, God will help them make the right choice.

# A Look at the Lesson

# Preparation

Gather a button; Bibles; a squirt bottle filled with water; a photocopy of the "Guide Me" handout; large bags of M&M's candy, raisins and peanuts; a large bowl; slips of paper; scissors; yellow and red construction paper; and a marker.

# 1 Hide the Button

(You'll need a button.)

Have kids form pairs. Ask one partner from each pair to leave the room for a moment. Have the remaining partners choose an obscure hiding place for the button, such as a child's pocket. Once the button is hidden, ask the kids outside the room to come back in.

Say: **While you were out, we hid a button. It's your job to find it.**

Let kids search for about 30 seconds. Then say: **Since you haven't found the button yet, I'm going to let your partner help. If you're getting close to where the button is, your partner will say "hot." If you're moving away, your partner will say "cold."**

Give a round of applause to the person who finds the button. Then ask:

● **How did it feel looking for the button with no help?**

88

● **How did it feel when your partner started helping you?**

Say: **Today we'll hear a story about a person who went looking for something very important and got some help along the way.**

## 2 A Difficult Task

(You'll need a Bible and a squirt bottle filled with water.)

Say: **Eventually the time came for Isaac to get married. In Bible times, parents often chose husbands and wives for their children. Abraham wanted to choose Isaac's wife from the country Abraham came from. But Abraham was very old—too old to travel there and choose the bride himself. So he decided to give the task to someone else.**

Ask for volunteers to be the reader, the servant and Rebekah. Have the rest of the students be camels. Say: **Listen carefully to the story so you can act out your parts.** Have the reader read Genesis 24:2-4.

Say: **The servant had a long journey ahead of him. So he loaded up several camels and started on his way.** Have the servant lead the camels around the classroom several times. **It was a long, hot journey.** Have the camels pant and roll their eyes. **Finally the town of Nahor came into sight. The servant knew he had a difficult task. So he went to the right place for help. Let's see what kind of help the servant asked for.**

As the reader reads Genesis 24:10-14, have the servant drop to his knees and fold his hands.

Say: **Let's see how God answered the servant's prayer.** Ask the reader to read Genesis 24:15 and 17-20. Hand the squirt bottle to Rebekah and have her give the servant and all the camels a squirt of water.

Say: **That's a pretty remarkable answer to prayer, isn't it? Rebekah took the servant to meet her family. The servant explained that he had come to find a wife for his master's son. He told about his prayer for guidance and how Rebekah had given him water for himself and for his camels. Let's see how Rebekah's family reacted.**

Have the reader read Genesis 24:50-53.

Say: **The next day Rebekah and the servant left to go back to the land of Canaan where Abraham and Isaac were waiting.** Have Rebekah and the servant lead the camels around the room in the opposite direction of their first journey. Say: **Now let's see if this story ends with a "happily ever after."**

Have the reader read Genesis 24:62-67.

# 3 God's Gracious Guidance

Ask:

● **How do you think the servant felt when Abraham asked him to find a wife for Isaac?**

● **Do you think he could have done it without God's help? Why or why not?**

● **How was trying to find the button without your partner's help like trying to find a wife for Isaac without God's help?**

● **What kind of prayer did the servant pray?**

● **Why were Rebekah and her family convinced that Rebekah should go back with the servant and become Isaac's wife?**

Ask for volunteers to tell about times they've prayed for and received God's guidance. Be prepared to share a story of God's guidance from your own life.

# 4 The Right Mix

(You'll need a photocopy of the "Guide Me" handout; three ingredients for trail mix: large bags of M&M's candy, peanuts and raisins; and a bowl.)

Form three groups. (A group may be as small as one or two people.) Give each group one of the stories from the "Guide Me" handout and have each group prepare a quick skit based on its story.

After each group presents its skit, ask:

● **How is God guiding the person in this situation?**

As you discuss the skits, help kids see that God uses circumstances, the Bible and other Christians to guide us. After each skit, as kids discover a new way God guides them, add one of the ingredients for trail mix to a bowl.

After discussing the skits and adding all three ingredients to the bowl, say: **Just as we used different ingredients to make our trail mix, God guides us with the right mix of clues. God may answer our prayers for guidance through circumstances, through the Bible, through other Christians or through a combination of all of these ways. Now, before we gobble up this trail mix, let's find out something else about God's guidance.**

# 5  Who Do You Trust?

(You'll need Bibles, slips of paper, the bowl of trail mix from the previous activity, scissors, yellow and red construction paper and a marker.)

Have kids remain in the three groups from the previous activity. Have one group remain in the room. Give the kids in that group Bibles and have them look up the following verses and mark them with slips of paper: Psalm 18:32; Psalm 25:9; Psalm 27:11; Psalm 31:3; Psalm 37:23.

Take the other two groups outside the room. Decide together where to hide the bowl of trail mix. As you hide the bowl, have one group cut small pieces of yellow construction paper and lay them in a path that leads to the hiding place.

Have the other group cut pieces of red construction paper and write "Fooled you!" on one piece. Have them lay the red pieces in a path that leads to the piece that says "Fooled you!"

When both paths have been marked, take the two groups back to the classroom.

Say to the group that remained in the room: **We've hidden the trail mix, but we've also left clues that tell where you can find it. We'll wait here while you search. When you find the trail mix, bring it back here and we'll eat it together.**

Let the other groups watch as the searching group looks for the trail mix. Don't let anyone give clues about which path to follow. When the searching group brings the trail mix back to the room, ask:

● **How did you feel when you saw there were two sets of clues?**

● **How did you know which path to follow?**

● **How did you feel when you got to the sign that said "Fooled you!" at the end of the red path?**

● **How is trying to decide which path to follow like trying to follow God's guidance when many of your friends aren't Christians?**

Say: **God gives us guidance about the right way to live. But sometimes we get messages from television and friends at school that tell us to go a different way. When we don't go God's way, sooner or later we'll run into a dead end, like the "Fooled you!" sign. It's really important to tune in to God's messages and tune out the rest.**

# 6 Pathfinders

(You'll need the bowl of trail mix and Bibles.)

Pass the trail mix around and let kids help themselves. Have the kids who marked the Bible verses take turns reading them aloud.

Ask:

● **What do these verses tell us about finding God's guidance?**

● **In what areas of our lives do we need to ask for God's guidance?**

Say: **When we need to make decisions, God's Word will always point us in the right direction. And when we go God's way** (point to the trail mix), **we know things will turn out for the best.**

# Guidance Prayers

Sit in a circle. Invite students to share their needs for guidance. Pair each person who has a need with another student who will be a prayer partner for that situation.

Close by praying: **Thank you, Lord, for promising to help us when we need to make decisions. Help us choose those things that show we love you and that we love others. Amen.**

# GUIDE ME

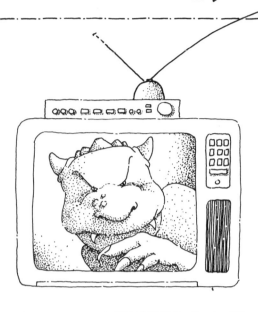

### Story 1
A person you've been trying to make friends with invites you and two other kids to a sleep-over. The friend says you're going to watch a really scary movie late at night. The other kids start talking about how fun that will be, but you're not sure you want to watch that kind of a movie. You don't know what to say or do. Then, on the day of the sleep-over you come down with a sore throat and fever.

### Story 2
Your parents bought you a bike helmet, but you don't like wearing it because none of your friends wear them. Two friends come by your house and ask you to ride with them to a park. You call your mom at work and ask her if you can go. She says yes. Neither of your friends is wearing a helmet and you're tempted not to wear yours, especially since your mom is at work and won't see you. Then you remember last week's lesson at church about honoring your parents.

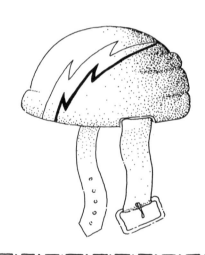

### Story 3
Several of your friends have been to church camp, and they always talk about how great it is. They love the crafts, horseback riding, canoeing and neat songs and speakers. It sounds fun, but you've never been away from your parents for a whole week and you're worried about getting homesick. You pray and ask God for guidance. The next week your favorite teacher from church tells you he's going to be one of the camp counselors and he hopes you'll be going to camp too.

# LESSON 13

## TRICKY OR TRUTHFUL?

**Story: Jacob Deceives Isaac**
**Genesis 25:21-34; 27:1–28:5**

Good News: Deceit and trickery separate us, but honesty draws us together.

Isaac and Rebekah had twin sons, Esau and Jacob. Because Esau was the firstborn, he was entitled to receive the birthright—a double share of the family property—and the blessing, which passed on the covenant promises of Abraham. Esau cared little for his inheritance and flippantly traded it for a bowl of stew. Then Rebekah conspired to trick Isaac into giving the paternal blessing to Jacob, her favorite, rather than Esau.

Though God had told Rebekah that the older son would serve the younger, she was not content to wait for God to accomplish this in his time. The deceit she and Jacob participated in resulted in pain and estrangement for the entire family. Third- and fourth-graders are sometimes tempted to shade the truth and manipulate people to gain their own ends. They need to see that deception always brings trouble in the end, while honesty and patience bring greater and more lasting rewards.

# A Look at the Lesson

1. **The Rich Boss** (10 minutes)
2. **Trade Me** (10 minutes)
3. **Who Am I?** (5-10 minutes)
4. **The Whole Truth** (10 minutes)
5. **Peacemakers** (5 minutes)
6. **Honest Prayers** (5 minutes)

# Preparation

Bake a frozen pizza and cut it into small squares. Arrange for an adult helper to bring it to you on your signal, about 15 minutes into the lesson. Gather slips of paper, pencils, small plastic bags, a few coins for each child, a small paper sack, blankets, a blindfold, a piece of fake fur, newsprint, markers and Bibles.

# The Rich Boss

(For each child you'll need a slip of paper, a pencil and a small plastic bag containing a few coins. You'll also need a small paper sack.)

Give each child a slip of paper, a pencil and a plastic bag containing a few coins. Ask:

● **How many of you would like to be rich?**

● **How many of you would like to be able to tell everyone else what to do?**

Have children write their names on the slips of paper, fold them and drop them in the paper sack.

Say: **The person whose name I draw from the sack will get to be the boss for a few minutes. You'll all have to give that person your bags of money and perform services for the boss such as bowing, scratching his or her back or singing a song.**

96

(Make sure that the boss doesn't ask a fellow student to do anything demeaning or embarrassing.)

As you prepare to pull a name from the bag, build excitement by having kids do a drumroll by slapping their legs. Once the boss has been chosen, have him or her sit on a chair in the middle of the room. Have the kids come forward one by one, hand the boss their bags of money, then perform whatever simple service the boss asks them to do.

After each person has come forward, tell the boss the game is over, take back the bags of money and ask:
- **How did it feel to be in charge?**
- **How did it feel to get everyone else's money?**
- **How did it feel to have to give the boss your money?**
- **How did it feel to have to perform services for the boss?**

Say: **Today's Bible story is about twin brothers who fought over who got to be the boss. But before we hear the story, let's make a tent to sit in.**

# 2 Trade Me

(You'll need blankets and a table. Arrange for a helper to bring the pizza squares on your signal.)

Have children help you assemble a tent by draping blankets over a large table. Then have everyone get inside the tent.

Say: **Now that we're all in here, I expect you to pay close a-TENT-tion! We made this tent because Isaac's family lived in tents. As this story begins, Isaac is an old man who's almost blind. He stays in his tent most of the time.**

**Isaac and Rebekah had twin sons, Esau and Jacob. They were fully grown men, and they were very different. Esau was a fiery, red-headed hunter. Jacob was a quiet man who liked to stay around the tents. Isaac loved Esau best. Esau was the oldest son, which meant that he would receive most of the land and a special blessing from Isaac. He would get to be the boss.**

**But Rebekah loved Jacob best. She wanted to see Jacob get the most land and the special blessing.**

**One day Esau had been out hunting. When he came home he was really hungry. He smelled something won-**

derful. **Jacob had been cooking a delicious stew.** Call for your helper to deliver the pizza to your tent. Hold the pizza in front of the children and ask them if it smells good.

Say: **Just imagine how good that stew smelled. Esau's stomach was growling. He said to Jacob, "Let me have some of that stew!" Jacob said, "First sell me your birthright." The birthright was very important—the son who had it would get twice as much land as the other son. But Esau said: "What good is my birthright when I'm dying of hunger? You can have it!"**

Invite children to share the pizza. Say: **So just like that, Esau traded away the land and power he would have had as the oldest son. But there was one more thing Esau could still have—the special blessing from his father.**

**Isaac knew that the time of his death was near. So he called Esau into his tent and said: "It's time for me to give you my blessing. Go hunting and bring me some tasty roasted meat. Then I'll give you my blessing."**

**Rebekah overheard her husband. So she called Jacob, her favorite son, and said: "I'll prepare some tasty goat meat. You take it to your father, then he'll give you the blessing instead of giving it to Esau."**

**Jacob said: "Esau is hairy, and I have smooth skin. My father will know I'm not Esau."**

**But Rebekah had everything planned. She covered Jacob's hands and neck with goatskins, so he would feel hairy like his brother. Then Jacob took the meal into his father. Isaac said: "You sound like Jacob, but you feel like Esau. Are you really Esau?"**

**Jacob lied and said, "I am." So Isaac gave the special blessing to Jacob. Soon after that, Esau came into the tent with the meat he had hunted and asked for his father's blessing. Isaac said: "Your brother tricked me. He took your blessing!"**

**Esau was so angry that he decided to kill Jacob. But Rebekah knew his plans and sent Jacob far away. Rebekah never saw her son Jacob again. Lies and tricks tore the family apart.**

# 3 Who Am I?

(You'll need a blindfold and a piece of fake fur.)

Have the children come out of the tent.

Say: **We're going to play a simple game to see how easy it was for Jacob to deceive Isaac.**

Blindfold a volunteer and have him or her sit in a chair. Put the piece of fake fur on another student's arm. Place the blindfolded child's hand on the fur-covered arm of the other student. Have the other student say, "I'm Esau." Then ask the blindfolded child to guess the other student's identity.

Give each student a chance to be the blindfolded guesser. Then bring everyone together and ask:

● **How do you feel when someone plays a trick on you?**

● **How do you think Isaac felt when he realized that Jacob had tricked him?**

● **How do you think Esau felt when he realized that his mother and brother had worked together to steal his blessing?**

● **Why do you think Jacob wanted the blessing?**

● **What happens when people in a family cheat each other and lie to each other?**

Say: **Lying or tricking people may help you get what you want, but there are always consequences to pay. Jacob got the birthright and the blessing, but he had to leave home for many years, live in fear of his brother and never see his parents again.**

# 4 The Whole Truth

(You'll need newsprint, markers and Bibles.)

Say: **Let's see what the Bible says about being honest.**

Form two groups. Give each group a sheet of newsprint, a marker and a Bible. Have one group look up Psalm 32:2 and write it on its newsprint. Have the other group look up and write Proverbs 2:6-7.

Say: **When you've finished writing your verses, tear your papers into several large pieces to make a puzzle.**

**Then you'll put together the other group's puzzle.**

As kids are writing their verses, quietly go to each group and whisper that they should hide one puzzle piece so the other group won't be able to finish the puzzle.

When groups are ready, have them switch puzzle pieces and work to complete the puzzles. When it becomes evident that each group has held back a puzzle piece, say: **What? You mean you tricked each other right here in church?** Ask:

● **How is this like the way people sometimes trick each other at home? at school?**

● **Why do people trick each other?**

Then say that you were the one who suggested the trickery, but now it's time to give each group the piece it needs to finish its puzzle. Have groups read their completed puzzles aloud. Ask:

● **What do these verses tell us about being honest?**

● **When is it tempting to be dishonest?**

## 5 Peacemakers

(You'll need the puzzle pieces from the previous activity.)
Say: **Each of you pick up a piece from one of the puzzles.**
Ask:

● **How do these torn pieces remind you of what happens when people lie and cheat?**

Say: **Friends and family get torn apart by lies and cheating. That's what happened to Jacob, and that's what still happens today. When it happens to us, Jesus wants us to be peacemakers.**

Ask:

● **What do peacemakers do?**

● **How can you be a peacemaker when someone lies to you or cheats you?**

Say: **It's not easy, but God wants us to be ready to forgive. Take your puzzle piece and turn it over to the blank side. Think of someone you need to forgive for lying to you, or someone you need to ask for forgiveness. Use your finger to write that person's name on your puzzle piece with invisible ink.**

# 6 Honest Prayers

(You'll need a blanket from the tent.)

Have kids sit close together on the floor. Bring one of the blankets from the tent and sit on the floor.

Say: **Jesus is always ready to forgive us and help us forgive others. His forgiveness covers us and protects us like a blanket.** As you continue to speak, have the children help you stretch the blanket over your heads. **His forgiveness brings angry, hurt people back together again. Let's pray for his forgiveness right now.**

**Dear Jesus, forgive us for the times we're not perfectly honest. And help us make peace with those who have been dishonest with us. Amen.**

# BRING THE BIBLE TO LIFE FOR YOUR 1ST THROUGH 6TH GRADERS... WITH GROUP'S HANDS-ON BIBLE CURRICULUM™

## Energize your kids with Active Learning!

Group's **Hands-On Bible Curriculum**™ will help you teach the Bible in a radical new way. It's based on Active Learning—the same teaching method Jesus used.

In each lesson, students will participate in exciting and memorable learning experiences using fascinating gadgets and gizmos you've not seen with any other curriculum. Your elementary students will discover biblical truths and <u>remember</u> what they learn because they're <u>doing</u> instead of just listening.

### You'll save time and money too!

While students are learning more, you'll be working less—simply follow the quick and easy instructions in the **Teachers Guide**. You'll get tons of material for an energy-packed 35- to 60-minute lesson. And, if you have extra time, there's an arsenal of Bonus Ideas and Time Stuffers to keep kids occupied—and learning! Plus, you'll SAVE BIG over other curriculum programs that require you to buy expensive separate student books—all student handouts in Group's **Hands-On Bible Curriculum** are photocopiable!

In addition to the easy-to-use **Teachers Guide**, you'll get all the essential teaching materials you need in a ready-to-use **Learning Lab**®. No more running from store to store hunting for lesson materials—all the active-learning tools you need to teach 13 exciting Bible lessons to any size class are provided for you in the **Learning Lab**.

### Challenging topics each quarter keep your kids coming back!

Group's **Hands-On Bible Curriculum** covers topics that matter to your kids and teaches them the Bible with integrity. Switching topics every month keeps your 1st- through 6th-graders enthused and coming back for more. The full two-year program will help your kids...
- make God-pleasing decisions,
- recognize their God-given potential, and
- seek to grow as Christians.

Take the boredom out of Sunday school, children's church, and youth group for your elementary students. Make your job easier and more rewarding with no-fail lessons that are ready in a flash. Order Group's **Hands-On Bible Curriculum** for your 1st- through 6th-graders today.

**Hands-On Bible Curriculum** is also available for Toddlers & 2s, Preschool, and Pre-K and K!

# TEACH YOUR PRESCHOOLERS AS JESUS TAUGHT WITH GROUP'S *HANDS-ON BIBLE CURRICULUM*™

**Hands-On Bible Curriculum™ for preschoolers** helps your preschoolers learn the way they learn best—by touching, exploring, and discovering. With active learning, preschoolers love learning about the Bible, and they really remember what they learn.

Because small children learn best through repetition, Preschoolers and Pre-K & K will learn one important point per lesson, and Toddlers & 2s will learn one point each month with **Hands-On Bible Curriculum**. These important lessons will stick with them and comfort them during their daily lives. Your children will learn:

- •God is our friend,
- •who Jesus is, and
- •we can always trust Jesus.

The **Learning Lab®** is packed with age-appropriate learning tools for fun, faith-building lessons. Toddlers & 2s explore big **Interactive StoryBoards**™ with enticing textures that toddlers love to touch— like sandpaper for earth, cotton for clouds, and blue cellophane for water. **Bible Big Books**™ captivate Preschoolers and Pre-K & K while teaching them important Bible lessons. With **Jumbo Bible Puzzles**™ and involving **Learning Mats**™, your children will see, touch, and explore their Bible stories. Each quarter there's a brand new collection of supplies to keep your lessons fresh and involving.

Fuzzy, age-appropriate hand puppets are also available to add to the learning experience. These child-friendly puppets help you teach each lesson with scripts provided in the **Teachers Guide**. Plus, your children will enjoy teaching the puppets what they learned. Cuddles the Lamb, Whiskers the Mouse, and Pockets the Kangaroo turn each lesson into an interactive and entertaining learning experience.

Just order one **Learning Lab** and one **Teachers Guide** for each age level, add a few common classroom supplies, and presto—you have everything you need to build faith in your children. For more interactive fun, introduce your children to the age-appropriate puppet who will be your teaching assistant and their friend. **No student books required!**

### Hands-On Bible Curriculum is also available for grades 1–6.

Order today from your local Christian bookstore, or write: Group Publishing, Box 485, Loveland, CO 80539.

# INNOVATIVE RESOURCES FOR YOUR CHILDREN'S MINISTRY

## Big Action Bible Skits
*Christine Yount*

At last—drama that's both exciting *and* easy! Using eight full-color overhead transparencies and ten skits, your elementary children will learn about the Bible as they act out favorite Old Testament Bible stories—without expensive scenery and sets. Simply shine the appropriate overhead on the wall and presto—instant staging!

Encourage learning by helping your children experience Bible stories...and have fun at the same time. Five- to 10-minute skits include...
- Adam and Eve,
- Noah and the Ark,
- Moses and the Exodus,
- Jonah and the Big Fish, and more!

ISBN 1-55945-258-7

## Helping Children Know God

A must for anyone who wants to help elementary-age children understand specific attributes of God. Here's active learning at its best—program ideas appeal to all five senses and include suggestions for use in and out of the classroom. You'll help children discover...
- God is loving
- God is faithful
- God is all-knowing
- God is everywhere...and more!

With 140 ideas for helping children know God, this book will be a part of your lesson planning week after week.

ISBN 1-55945-605-1

## 101 Creative Worship Ideas for Children's Church
*Jolene Roehlkepartain*

Get your children excited about God with over 100 new, creative ideas for children's worship. Each idea is easy to use and works for children's church, Sunday school, or any place children are gathered to worship God.

You'll discover ideas for...
- prayers
- devotions
- puppet scripts
- object lessons
- Bible stories
- holidays, and more!

Written by children's ministry veteran Jolene Roehlkepartain, this book is jam packed with creative ideas that will help you lead your children in worship meetings that are exciting and meaningful.

ISBN 1-55945-601-9

Order today from your local Christian bookstore, or write:
Group Publishing, Box 485, Loveland, CO 80539.